Dear Zelda®

Other books by Carol Gardner and Shane Young

Zelda Wisdom

The Zen of Zelda

Zelda Rules on Love

Zelda's Survival Guide

Zelda's Tips from the Tub

Zelda's Bloopers

Zelda's Moments with Mom

Also by Carol Gardner

Bumper Sticker Wisdom

Dear Zelda,

Carol Gardner and Shane Young

A Zelda Wisdom® Book

**Andrews McMeel
Publishing, LLC**

Kansas City

07 08 09 10 11 TWP 10 9 8 7 6 5 4 3 2 1

ISBN-13: 978-0-7407-6051-8
ISBN-10: 0-7407-6051-3

Library of Congress Control Number: 2006932201

www.andrewsmcmeel.com

Attention: Schools and Businesses

Andrews McMeel books are available at quantity discounts with bulk purchase for educational, business, or sales promotional use. For information, please write to: Special Sales Department, Andrews McMeel Publishing, LLC, 4520 Main Street, Kansas City, Missouri 64111.

Advice: It's more fun to give than to receive.

—Malcolm Forbes

A Little Tough but Tender Advice

When a friend first suggested I write an advice column I was taken aback. To my knowledge, no dog has ever written an advice column. Actually, we dogs don't write much at all. But the more I thought about it, the more I realized that I was qualified, in part because I've been dishing out dollops of wisdom all my life through my cards and books. We do call the company "Zelda Wisdom" after all. It turns out I'm even accredited: No other dog has ever received an Honorary "Pet" Degree from Harvard University (even if it was from their Dining Services). But make no bones about it, a Harvard degree is a Harvard degree, even when it comes from their kitchen.

Harvard University Dining Services

By authority of the Executive Chef and in gratitude for your enthusiastic participation in the Recipes from Home program, I hereby confer upon

Zelda Gardner
the honorary position of

Chief Pie Taster

with all weight gain, strawberry breath and dental disease thereof. Please accept our greatest appreciation (and a scratch behind the ear). Given in Cambridge, Massachusetts this Nineteenth day of April, Nineteen Hundred Ninety-Nine.

D. Michael Miller
D. Michael Miller
Executive Chef

Giving advice isn't always easy, but then again, giving it is often easier than getting it! As Oscar Wilde said, "The only thing to do with good advice is pass it on. It is never of any use to oneself." I certainly do like to pass it on, but little did I know how entertaining, touching, inspiring, and fun it would be to hear these stories. Every day I get letters and e-mails from all parts of the world. It seems no region is without problems, and everyone can use a little nice advice now and again. From "Horny in Hong Kong" to "Lonely in Los Angeles," thousands of people have sent us inquiries. We can only hope that somewhere out there we've made a difference or at the very least that "Horny in Hong Kong" and "Lonely in Los Angeles" might have the chance to meet up someday.

Before getting to the letters, I want to take a minute to thank those members of Team Zelda who've assisted in researching and writing the *Dear Zelda* column (my paws often have a hard time with the keys). When I needed info on dealing with bullies and other heavy problems, Wendy Frank came to my rescue. When we received inquiries for tips on shopping, or when we needed some extra sleuthing, Susan Hauser gave me a helping hand. And when I was stumped for advice on doggy adoption or the newest puppy haute couture, Ron Giusti was there for me. Along the way, Jay Gardner used his talents as a writer and editor to assist with the end results for many of my columns. I put my paw print on the final drafts, but without the help of these folks, the advice would not be half as good.

I hope you will enjoy this collection of our favorite *Dear Zelda* columns. If you're hungry for more, check out the weekly column at www.zeldawisdom.com. And always remember to be discerning in *who* you ask for advice . . . some are wise, and some are otherwise. With this many wrinkles, trust me, I must be wise.

Zelda

A Broad . . . Vacationing

Practice safe packing . . . when in doubt leave it out.

Dear Zelda

My boyfriend and I have a lot in common but are polar opposites when it comes to traveling. I like to relax, sit by a pool, or lie on the beach, enjoy a margarita or two, and chill. He always wants to go go go and visit every tourist attraction. When the vacation is over, I need a vacation from our vacation.
What can I do?

Travelin' a Go-Go

Dear Travelin' a Go-Go,

For starters, trade in the go-go boots for a good pair of no-no boots. Put your foot down and let him know that you're on vacation, too. Polar opposites are okay, but from the sound of it, you two are practically bipolar opposites! How does it happen that months in advance you plan the same trip, take the same time off, and yet once you get there your ideas of relaxation leave you both "sole" survivors? Sorry, girlfriend, if you two are going on vacation together, you're going to have to try on a pair of sensible sneakers (I know . . . not nearly as stylish as an "all about me" pair of sling-back heels, but at least those toes know what they're slipping into before they leave).

Next time you're planning to travel together, set the style before you go. You need rest—he needs the sites. If you can, figure this out in advance so you can eliminate the ol' vacation tug-of-war. Try on a compromise that fits both your needs. Go on his hike (burns calories for an extra margarita), marvel at the patina on a few old statues (could inspire a paint color for your guest room), and snorkel with a sea lion (you're on your own there). In return, he gives you the space to lounge by the pool in a teeny bikini, fruity beverage in tow. You'll end up with a "pretty pedi," free of those cumbersome, guilt-laced, out-of-style go-go boots. Are you ready, boots? Start walkin'.

Zelda

Aging

Go BRALESS . . . it pulls the wrinkles down!

Dear Zelda,

My husband and I have been married for the past ten years. We are both well into our forties with a little bit of gray starting to show, and of course my husband looks dashing and distinguished while I look "old and matronly." We live out on a farm where we don't get to see many people and although my husband thinks I look "great," I'm not feeling it. I feel like I look . . . OLD. I'm afraid he'll start to wander toward greener pastures. How do you keep your ageless appearance?

Hi Ho Silver!

Dear Hi Ho Silver!

Well, I certainly appreciate the compliment. Then again, when you're born looking like a furry raisin, there's nowhere to go but up! And don't let my so-called perfection fool you—even I require effort to look this good! We're talking assistants, makeup artists, a great wardrobe, subtle mood lighting, and the one thing all us aging beauties *have* to have . . . the Joan Collins soft-focus lens on our camera.

You're only as old as you feel. Your attitude, as well as the face you put forward, reveals so much more about you than your years, your wrinkles, or your hair color. The point is, maybe your inner and outer selves have fallen out of sync. But never fear! A subtle change may be all you need to put that spring back in your step. It could be as simple as touching up your gray or trying a new hairstyle, or, if you want to try something bigger, think about beginning a yoga or art class, starting a new hobby, or planning and taking a trip with your husband. Just don't go overboard and show up at dinner in a miniskirt with extra helpings of hairspray and rouge . . . you're going for Hi Ho Silver, not the silver high ho.

Find healthy ways to build your confidence and define your own strong, independent identity as you age, and you will discover the closest thing to a fountain of youth that exists. Most important, reread what you just wrote me: Your husband thinks you look *great*! The next time he compliments you, instead of shaking your head or downplaying it, take a deep breath, smile, and say, "Thank you."

Trust me, we all age. But that's not always a bad thing, as long as we try to do it gracefully, with a little humor and lots of backlighting. Hi Ho Silver, away!

Zelda

Annoying Neighbors

Sorry neighbor, Mr. Rogers doesn't live here anymore.

Dear Zelda,

My wife and I recently moved into a new home in a nice neighborhood. One day my wife was in the bathroom. She had just stepped out of the shower and, as she glanced in the mirror, was shocked to see our neighbor's face in the window staring at her. Since then she repeatedly sees him patrolling outside our bathroom window. He and his wife seem nice enough and have even invited us over for a neighborhood barbecue. We don't know what to do about this Peeping Tom next door. Any suggestions?

Nervous Neighbor

Dear Nervous Neighbor,

As Mr. Rogers liked to say, "It's a beautiful day in the neighborhood." What he forgot to mention was, "Unless your neighbor is a creepy peeper." Peeping Toms have long been treated as laughable individuals—a little strange, but often considered harmless. This is absolutely wrong; violations of privacy are serious. Seeing Mr. Won't-You-Be-My-Neighbor staring back at her must have been frightening and humiliating for your wife.

I have a couple of ideas for you. First, wait until your neighbor isn't home, then let his wife know in a pleasant but concerned tone that . . . gasp, there is a Peeping Tom in your neighborhood. Tell her everyone is on the lookout, and that when "Tom" is found he will be tarred, feathered, and displayed in the cul-de-sac. My guess is she will share this information with her husband, and that will be the end of it. If he continues, try putting a motion-sensitive camera in the bathroom facing the window to catch him in the act, preferably multiple times. Then talk to him privately, show him the evidence, and tell him that your next step will be to call the authorities if he doesn't desist.

For general peace of mind, you might consider peeper-proofing your bathroom window by installing opaque glass or adding a thick curtain. Even if your neighbor quits peeping, you might feel more comfortable in the bathroom, and it's cheap and easy to make these changes.

Don't take your neighbor's voyeurism lightly. If he continues peeping, or if you suspect he's a threat, call the police. Voyeurism is invasive, wrong, and illegal. It's too bad that jeepers, creepers, your peeper lives next door.

Zelda

Babies and Puppies

Have buggy . . . let's boogie. Baby in charge.

Dear Zelda,

My sister is the mother of a two-year-old monster. Last week we were having lunch in Denny's and her little boy started screaming because he wanted to leave the table and run around. As usual, she gave in to him, and finally the manager came and politely asked her to either keep her son, who at this point was pouring salt on the floor, at the table or leave. My sister got mad at the manager and we left the restaurant without finishing our meal. I don't want to tell her how to raise her son, but she is creating a monster. What should I do?

Sister in Distress

Dear Sister in Distress,

When a two-year-old gets kicked out of Denny's, something's amiss with the parenting. The fact that your sister let it happen is troubling. A two-year-old should never be in control of his mother. But how do you do anything about it without insulting or alienating your sister?

It might be hard, and foolish, to bluntly say, "You are the mother of a two-year-old monster, and he's behaving that way because of you." My suggestion is to invite your sister to lunch . . . alone. Take her to a busy fast-food restaurant with a lot of young children. Look for out-of-control kiddies, and choose a table close to the worst offenders. Let your sister see those children as examples of parental failure, and hope that it sparks a conversation on the subject. You may not feel comfortable telling your sister how to discipline *her* son, but you can sure let loose on the behavior of *other* out-of-control kiddies.

When your nephew goes to school he will be faced with rules enforced by his teachers, and unless he has opportunities to be mature, responsible, and compassionate now, he will not have the social skills he needs later to be the best that he can be in school and in life. Excessive permissiveness rarely helps children grow up, and often produces just the opposite . . . emotionally immature adults.

Of course, it seems everybody knows how to raise children, except the people who have them. Thus, in your case you might just want to share a couple of great books with your sister: *Love and Logic Magic for Early Childhood: Practical Parenting from Birth to Six Years* and *Helicopters, Drill Sergeants, and Consultants: Parenting Styles and the Messages They Send*, both by Jim Fay. They will give your sis some practical parenting skills with an upbeat, sensible approach. Now you just need to figure out a way to sneak them into her bag when she's not looking! Here's to turning your distress into success.

Zelda

Bad Company

It's better to be alone than to be in bad company.

Dear Zelda,

My best friend and I work in management for a large retail clothing chain, and two weeks ago I was promoted and now am her boss. Up until then we pretty much did everything together from high school to college to now. All of a sudden she's busy all the time, and she always jokes (in a nonjoking way) that I'm the big boss and she needs to be careful. I don't even know what that means. I'm really sad about it, but I work really hard and I do want to excel at my job and move up with the company. I feel like I've been fired from our friendship. Help!

Friendship GAP

Dear Friendship GAP,

Congrats on the promotion! In today's competitive work environment, getting a promotion is a *really big deal* and reinforces the fact that your company values your talent and abilities. You should feel no need to apologize for your hard work or for the rewards you reap.

It's time for your best friend to lose the bargain-basement attitude. The jealousy routine is not appropriate, especially at work, and especially if she's your best friend. Promotions are the natural offshoot of hard work, but unfortunately your best friend sees this as a blow to her ego instead of kudos to you for your performance. You may be her boss, but there will always need to be a mutual amount of R-E-S-P-E-C-T between the T-W-O of you in order for the friendship to continue.

That said, it's up to you, in the position of power, to make her understand that her friendship is still size XL (my favorite size!) in your book. But go easy on her. You can give her attitude a dressing down without putting her down. Try leaving behind the confines of sales, price checks, and spring halters, and invite her out for coffee or a drink. Even if she claims she's busy, persevere and find a time she can't manage to refuse. Spending time together outside of work will hopefully remind her why you were best friends to begin with.

If that's not enough, have an honest talk about your concerns and why you feel your friendship has changed. Don't be accusatory; be sensitive to her feelings of insecurity about your promotion. Let her know how important her friendship is and that your relationship runs deeper than any job-related issues. Fortunately, you've built up a steady reserve of good memories and shared experiences, which should allow you to weather this storm. Sometimes all it takes is a simple gesture to stir up fond memories and light the sparks in an old friendship. Good luck!

Zelda

Back to School

They told me cheerleaders always get a quarterback . . .
I didn't even get a dime.

Dear Zelda,

My daughter is going off to college in the beginning of September and my husband and I will be empty nesters. I'm going to miss her presence and the constant flow of her friends coming in and out of our house. My stomach aches every time I think about her leaving. I keep a smile on my face but inside my heart is breaking. What do I do to ease the pain?

Empty Nester

Dear Empty Nester,

What a wonderful thing to be able to send your daughter off to college, where she will broaden her horizons, develop her own ideas and identity, and continue her journey into the world of adulthood. She'll have new friends to make, new places to see, and new stories to tell when she comes home. Of course, these departures can cause real heartbreak for the parents, but in addition, they're also a chance for a long-overdue and well-deserved "kid break"!

Stop and take a deep breath. Let's put a different spin on this daughter-leaving business. It's obvious you love her, but it's time to push her from the nest. You've given her wings. Now let her fly. Your mother had to do it, and her mother before that. No one said it would be easy, but this is the natural cycle of things. She is not the only one taking flight; you are, too! Be strong. Whether she tells you or not, she's counting on it, and whether she shows it or not, it's hard for her, as well. Let her know that you will miss her greatly, but try not to burden her with your own separation woes. After all, you are only a cell call, text message, or e-mail away.

Now, to ease the pain . . . hmmmmmmm . . . let me think here. I can only come up with about *five hundred* things you can do. Make a list of the things you've always wanted to do but couldn't because you were busy playing "soccer mom," or "mom taxi," or better yet . . . "mom the maid." Throw some ceramic pots, join a book club, or learn a new language. I'm not talking about trying to replace her. Just think of this as your next "major" in the college of life. And this time you get to take all the fun classes! Turn that empty nest into a launching pad!

Zelda

Bad Habits

If something smells fishy . . . it probably is!

Dear Zelda,

My husband and I are newlyweds. We both work at nine-to-five jobs, and I cook dinner for us every night. When my husband gets home from work, the first thing he does is turn on the television, even before he asks about my day. When we eat dinner he leaves the news on and as soon as dinner is over he expects me to clean up while he returns to a big easy chair and the TV. I feel like "the honeymoon is over" and I'm not liking the reality of our new married relationship. Help! What should I do to bring a little romance back to our marriage?

Married to the Television

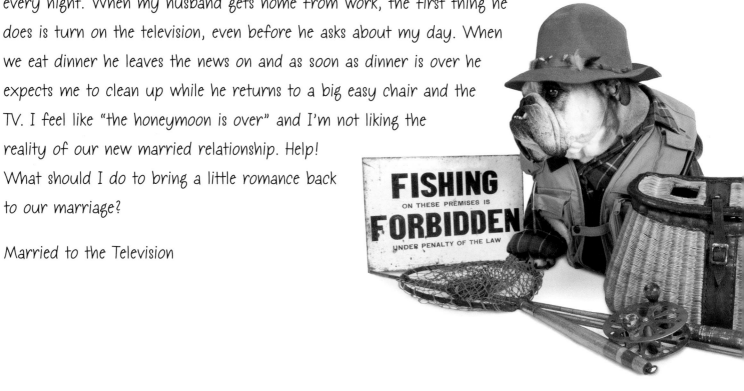

Dear Married to the Television,

Congratulations are in order on the new nuptials, but I'm sorry to hear that the groom is forty-two inches wide and displays over five hundred channels. I'm sure he looked a lot better in a tuxedo at the altar. Why are you the one stuck making the dinner every night *and* cleaning up . . . aren't relationships supposed to be fifty-fifty? You may be right that the relationship needs an injection of some new romance, but first it needs a good dose of respect.

Grab that remote! This is your marriage . . . make sure it doesn't become just a miniseries! "Give and take" are the two stars of a more perfect union, and that means give and take between *both* of you. If all he sees over his elbow macaroni is the evening news, turn it off. It's easy to settle into a comfortable routine without realizing that you're both watching very different channels. This is the time to fine-tune all those little things that need fine-tuning. Better to fix problems now than become resentful over them for years to come. The honeymoon isn't over; it's just on a first-season hiatus.

Start with one simple rule: no TV dinners. Enjoy one another, talk, and just share some peace and quiet. He may love his "TV on Demand," but he needs to listen to your "TV Off!" demand for at least an hour every night. And if you go out to eat, avoid those trendy movie houses where you can eat pizza, drink beer, and watch a movie. Unless he's sportin' VHF reception through his wedding band, try sitting outside, commercial-free, breathing in fresh romance while breathing out bad reception.

The viewers have spoken . . . you don't belong on *Divorce Court* just yet, and your marriage may turn out to be a Lifetime Original.

Zelda

Breaking Up

Remember the alimony!

Dear Zelda,

I am a middle-aged woman and have been dating a man for several weeks. If I were to make a list of qualities that I desire in a man, he would be perfect. The problem is that I don't feel any "sparks" or attraction to him. We have some interests in common and enjoy each other's company, and I would like to have a platonic relationship. He is a romantic and is already thinking of exotic vacations together. I have not done anything to mislead him and have been direct in communicating that I want a friendship with him. I don't want to hurt his feelings, but I don't see us as a "couple." How should I explain this to him without hurting his feelings or having him feel rejected?

Uncomfortable One

Dear Uncomfortable One,

We all are familiar with the saying "love is blind," but what happens when "love is hearing-impaired"?

There's an unwritten rule that all relationships have a sort of "trial period" when one begins dating. The trial period, or as I like to call it the "Do I or don't I?" period is when both parties evaluate the "spark" potential. Don't underestimate the value of the spark. Sparks are the fuel that ignite the fire, and if they aren't there now, they aren't likely to show up later. Settle for a relationship without them and you'll just end up being two sticks rubbin' each other the wrong way.

Too many relationships end bitterly because one or both partners allow the relationship to advance without understanding what is missing. Honesty is still the winner when it comes to any relationship, romantic or platonic. Unfortunately, for some people, *not* saying something is another way of actually "saying something else." You may be telling him that you want a "friendship" with him, but have you actually told him that you *don't* have romantic feelings for him? Without adding the last part of that sentence, he may be thinking that the "friendship" is just the beginning of a relationship yet to blossom, and that given time, the friendship will become courtship.

Situations like this are best met head-on: up-front and personal. This is not easy. Be strong, be honest, and be sure not to send any mixed signals, even though you want to be nice and not hurt him. You've only been dating a few weeks, and as irresist-a-bull as you are, I'm sure he will survive, and you may even manage to become friends. It will save both of you a lot of heartache in the long run.

It may not feel great to throw water on his fire, but without feeling any heat from you, his flame is sure to fizzle out, too. Be strong!

Zelda

Bullying

Life is tough . . . wear a helmet.

Dear Zelda,

My daughter gets off the bus in tears and has
nightmares because she is regularly bullied by other girls
in her junior high school. Her grades have dropped, and
some days she even pleads to stay home. These mean
girls tease her about her accent and her clothes. How
can I help my daughter so she won't be so miserable?

Clueless

Dear Clueless,

Your daughter joins more than 160,000 students who miss school on any given day because of the fear of being bullied. At home you might role-play with her to teach her assertiveness and confidence boosters like "Life is tough, but you're tougher." Invite friends over to play the board game Block the Bully Cycle (Franklin Learning Systems), which teaches children to stop bullying, whether they find themselves the target, the bystander, or the bully. Suggest that the school's principal set aside a Bullying Stops Here Awareness Week as the first ste in transforming the campus into a bully-free zone. The book *Bullies and Victims: Helping Your Child Survive the Schoolyard Battlefield* by SuEllen Fried and Paula Fried might be a valu-a-bull resource.

    I used to get depressed when I'd hear people making fun of the fact that I dress up in silly outfits, drool, and have an underbite orthodontists dream about. I've learned to like who I am and to be happy with it. Comfort and listen to your daughter. Tell her how wonderful she is. This will be the first step in helping your daughter bully-proof herself. She deserves your help.

Zelda

Competition

You don't have to be ruthless to be competitive.

Dear Zelda,

There is a coworker in my office who always seems to get the attention from my boss and the men in the office. She is very attractive and whenever I'm around her, I feel less-than-secure in myself. I just think I can never be as "wonderful, beautiful, smart, and sexy" as little "Miss Perfect." It's just so frustrating. How do I work with her without feeling like the ugly stepsister? (By the way, I'm fit, fun, and not so bad to look at.)

Miss Not-So-Perfect

Dear Miss Not-So-Perfect,

You feel like an ugly stepsister . . . yet you say, "I'm fit, fun, and not so bad to look at." Hate to say it girl, but you're sounding less like an "ugly stepsister" and more like a "glaring contradiction–sister."

You seem to have a lot going for you . . . the trick is to realize it! Being jealous of a coworker because she's beautiful and gets a lot of attention is a little too "sibling rivalry" for the workplace, but it's incredibly common. There's nothing wrong with wanting to feel attractive, but if you want to compete with this boardroom bombshell, you need to impress your colleagues with your skills as a professional, not just with your assets . . . elsewhere.

Build up confidence in both yourself and your work, and in no time at all you'll go from middle-management Miss Not-So-Perfect to multinational management maven. Sure, a tight sweater gets attention, and a hair flip or giggle can garner a few groupies, but those qualities will look like window-dressing the day you score the big account for your company, cut expenses by half, or come up with that fabulous new marketing idea that grabs the boss's attention.

Ultimately, results speak louder than looks. Your comely counterpart is not to blame for what the good Lord gave her. Like you, she's using what she's got, and despite the veneer of success, she is probably just as insecure as you are. Take a few memos on the things you *do* like about her and try to incorporate some of those traits into your own style. (Just don't go overboard . . . it can get creepy quickly, and we've all seen *Single White Female*!)

Bottom line: Do your best to see people as people. Once you let your guard down and gain some confidence in your own ability, you may find that this brainy beauty becomes the office "sister you never had."

Zelda

Cosmetic Surgery

Face-lift? . . . Do you think anyone will notice?

Dear Zelda,

My stepdaughter, who is beautiful, has informed her dad and me that all she wants for graduation from high school is a bigger set of breasts. I admit that she isn't the biggest of the bunch, but they're not the smallest, either. Mine are about the same size and I've done just fine all these years. It's not the money that concerns me (her dad and I promised her a trip that costs about that much), but more the fact that I would be condoning something that I personally don't believe in. She will be eighteen and able to start making those decisions without our consent. Her mother died ten years ago and I feel like the evil stepmother who isn't "cool." Any words of wisdom?

Topsy-Turvy

Dear Topsy-Turvy,

Our culture bombards us with messages and bad role models suggesting that bustiness is next to godliness. Big breasts are *everywhere*, and while big can be beautiful (as can small!), the national obsession with overinflated chests is too much hot air. Let's hope cup size doesn't start "popping up" on résumés any time soon or, for that matter, in latte sizes . . . "I'd like a double mocha latte in a size D cup, please."

Yes, your stepdaughter is an adult and legally can make her own decisions. You don't want to come off as the wicked-witch-of-a-stepmom, but you're still her parents, and as the underwriters of this extreme makeover, you *definitely* have final say in what your money is used for.

Your stepdaughter is still young, and her body has probably not finished developing yet. She may decide in the long run that she'd like to have a little more heavage in her cleavage, but now is *not* the time. Aside from the psychological impact, it doesn't make sense physically: It can be risky, the changes are permanent, and what seems like a great idea at eighteen may not seem (or look) so hot three or four operations later at age twenty-eight, or thirty-eight, or forty-eight.

I respect your desire to treat your stepdaughter as an adult. Parenting is about knowing when to let your children make their own mistakes and learn from them. But some mistakes are permanent, and sometimes it pays to be the uncool stepmom. She'll thank you in the long run.

Zelda

Dating and Mating

Ladybug looking for a manbug . . . know any?

Dear Zelda,

I am dating a great guy who has a big rottweiler. My problem is that my sweet little cocker spaniel doesn't like his big old rottweiler, and we can't go anywhere with the two of them. We would like to go camping but can't imagine having them in the same car together, let alone the same tent. Any advice would be helpful, Zelda.

Canines Cramping Camping

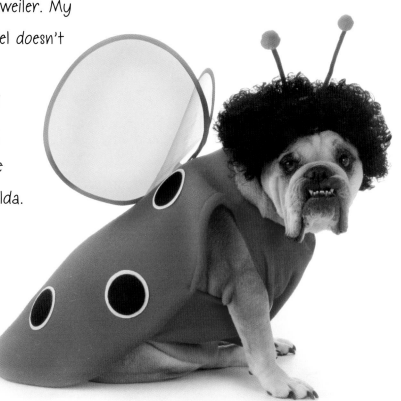

Dear Canines Cramping Camping,

The most important advice I can offer is to "pack" before you leave. By "pack," I'm not talking burgers and bug spray; I'm talking about establishing the pack order of your two dogs. I'd bet your cocker spaniel and his rottweiler didn't meet on neutral territory. This happened to Zoe and me. We were introduced in *my* home and because it was my turf, when she walked in, the fur flew and a lot of canine four-letter words were exchanged, especially when puppy Zoe decided to jump on *my* bed. It took a long time to straighten out the pack order, not to mention the rest of the house.

My first suggestion is to reintroduce your dogs (both on leashes) in a neutral location, like an enclosed park or yard neither dog has previously visited. That's how I met ZeeZee, and once we established rank (*me me me*) by sniffing, peeing, tail-wagging, and growling, I couldn't wait to bring ZeeZee home. If one of your dogs becomes overly aggressive, separate them and reprimand the aggressor. Comfort both dogs, but be firm. Have them "sit" for a little time-out and then try again. Continue to shorten the distance between the two dogs, letting them sort out their position in the pack.

Once your dogs have established their pack order, only then is it time to bring them home. (If you are living in two homes you'll need to do this twice.) I strongly suggest that you let the "other" dog enter first to reduce the chance that your dog feels the need to protect her/his turf. Keep both dogs on loose leashes for the first few days so you can grab and quickly correct unacceptable behavior. You might have two separate crates, separate bowls and toys, and definitely two separate sleeping areas until they are comfortable with each other. Feed them in separate areas, too. Soon it will be obvious which dog is the alpha, so feed that dog first and continue to recognize his/her alpha status.

Be sure to confine them to separate areas when you are away. Most important, never leave the dogs alone together until they have accepted each other, and even then, do so with caution. Be consistent in following my advice, and it won't be long before your sleeping bags are bundled, your camp stove is stowed, and your car is crowded with companionable canines.

Here's to happy s'mores and snores.

Zelda

Deception

Beware of "woofs" . . . in sheep's clothing.

Dear Zelda,

My "boyfriend" and I have been dating for almost a month now. We've been spending quite a lot of time together but I have yet to meet even one of his friends, coworkers, family members, or his roommate. We are always at my apartment because his roommate is a total slob (according to him). Even though I say I don't mind the mess, he still says, "Nah, your place is cleaner and cozier." I can't call him at work, and he can only be reached via his cell phone. Am I being naive here or is this guy really a "wolf in sheep's clothing"?

Astray from the Flock

Dear Astray from the Flock,

Insecurity comes with the territory of a new relationship. It's normal to ask yourself, "Does he like me as much as I like him?" And everyone at one time or another wonders, "Does he want to take this to the next level, or is he scared of commitment?"

But when we get into "Does he have a girlfriend or a wife?" "Is Larry his real name?" and "Is he an undercover CIA operative?" things get a little fishy. His evasiveness and secrecy are really not normal, and you are right to want to get to the bottom of this case before getting involved any further.

I'm going to give you two options: the ninja option and the real option. Let's talk about the fun one first. Get yourself some camouflage makeup, a tight black outfit (think DKNY meets kung fu), and the DVD of *Mission Impossible*. Then physically and mentally prepare yourself for a full-scale assault on the truth behind your beau. Set up some surveillance—or trail him from your house—and find out what the rest of his day is all about, if he really goes home to a wife and kids, or if his roommate is actually a slob.

But wait . . . this is *real life*, not the movies. More important, this is a relationship based (hopefully) on trust, so the worst thing you could do is spy on and deceive this person with whom you are trying to build an honest partnership.

Instead, you should try something even scarier . . . asking for the truth. There's nothing wrong with wanting to see where he lives, meet his friends, or break bread with his relatives. Let him know that this is important to you and be willing to draw the line firmly: Tell him that if he is not able to compromise on some of this stuff you will be forced to doubt either his honesty or his commitment to you. He may just be slow to warm up, so be patient with him but stay firm on your principles. You're worth it, sister!

Don't underestimate your suspicions and your intuition. Ultimately you will know deep down whether you trust him or not, and it's that gut feeling you should follow.

Zelda

Dieting
Practically Svelte

Dear Zelda,

We've really appreciated your good remarks in the past. My husband and I are both trying to lose weight and not succeeding too well. I've lost up to about fifty pounds several times in the past and then regained it and more, but I would sure appreciate some help staying on course now.

Your Admirers

Dear Admirers,

Thanks for your good-to-my-ears comment. I used to think that inside me was a skinny dog just trying to get out. I found I could usually keep her quiet with cookies, but that wasn't a good solution to my weight problem.

You and your husband can be each other's coach and motivator (not watchdog). Losing fifty pounds is commend-a-bull. Look upon your past weight loss attempts as a learning experience, not a failure. Discover what triggers you to eat by keeping a food diary, and chart your accompanying events and emotions. Have a steady diet of exercising more and eating less. Here are my suggestions for do-a-bull healthy habits:

- Place a picture of your slimmer self on your refrigerator next to your weight-loss goals.
- If you don't have a dog, adopt one and take her/him for daily walks.
- Never food shop when your stomach is growling.
- Instead of movie dates, go on "moving dates" (bike, bowl, hike, golf).
- Walk on a treadmill while watching your favorite television show.
- Get a cordless phone and walk while talking on it . . . even if you walk in circles.
- Wear clothes that are a little too tight. When it's uncomfortable to eat, you'll eat less.
- Avoid fast foods, soda, and the candy aisle in the market.
- Don't woof down your food or lick your plate clean.
- Drink lots of water, and then some more.
- Eat plenty of high-fiber foods and foods that are rich in water (fruits, veggies, broth-based soups).
- Get enough Zzzzzzzs.
- When you both reach your weight-loss goals, reward each other with a day-spa certificate or an active vacation.

Exercising and keeping the weight off will give you a new leash on life. I can't think of better incentives to stay the course . . . unless your class reunion's coming up. Stick together, slim together, and smooch together. A kiss burns nine calories. Indulge.

Zelda

Diversity

How can you choose sides on a round planet?

Dear Zelda,

I am a single mother of two elementary school girls. Although I was born in Mexico, I grew up in Los Angeles. One of my daughters is being harassed by some children in her class who call her "Un-American." My daughter comes home in tears and doesn't want to go to school. It breaks my heart. What should I tell her that would help her survive in school?

Mom in Misery

Dear Mom in Misery,

I remember being a pup myself, and let me tell you, it wasn't all days at the beach. Some other dogs at the playground would call me "Un-American" just because I'm an English bulldog! And there's *no one* more American than I am. So I sympathize with you and your daughter's plight; it is unfortunate and unfair.

Kids often say things they don't understand or don't mean, but it doesn't take away the sting and the hurt. We tend to look back on our own elementary school experiences with rose-colored glasses, and it's easy to forget that it's a dog-eat-dog world in school! Kids can be particularly cruel to anyone they consider different, whether it's because of their looks, their speech, or even something as simple as what they bring for lunch. What's even worse (and even scarier) is the possibility that children are learning this type of behavior from their parents, which is simply un-accept-a-bull. In either case, you need to speak to your daughter's teacher to find out more about these children. Are they teasing other students? Have they done this before? If so, the teacher may be able to address the situation at school either with the principal or with the parents.

As for what you should say to your daughter . . . that's a little tougher. All parents want to protect their children and fight their battles for them, especially when they are being treated unfairly and hurtfully. Unfortunately, all you can do is reassure your daughter that she is as American as it gets, and that she should be proud of her multicultural heritage. While other parents might teach their children hurtful and hateful things, you can be sure that *you* teach your daughter the values of tolerance and understanding, as well as strength of character, even in the face of discrimination and prejudice. While this may not immediately remedy the situation at hand, you can be proud of raising a sensitive and kind human being. Now *that* is truly an American legacy. Good luck, sister!

Zelda

Divorce

Love, honor, and negotiate

Dear Zelda,

My wife and I recently separated and are going through a divorce. We both want our dog, Harvey. How can we solve this dilemma? We need your canine counseling.

Almost Single

Dear Almost Single,

On behalf of all the canine pets of this world, thanks for asking this question. One dog has never been divisible by two. Harvey's well-being should rank above either of your wants. Being tossed back and forth like a Frisbee would be disorienting and destabilizing for any four-legged critter. Even if you go for joint custody, this doesn't have to mean joint physical custody or equal-time custody. Negotiate which one of you could ensure Harvey adequate dog support: time/attention, daily exercise, medical care, good kibbles, comfortable quarters, and a loving, stable environment. Permit the other one visiting and field-trip rights.

   Doggy heaven forbid if you can't come to a mutually accept-a-bull solution. *The Divorce Sourcebook* by Dawn Bradley Berry might offer you some insights and assist with other snarly settlement issues. Never divorce yourselves from Harvey's feelings and needs. This could be grounds for bad canine karma.

Zelda

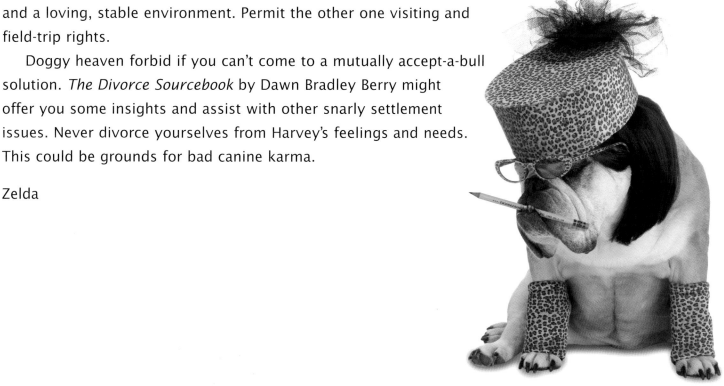

Dog Days of Summer

Let it all hang out, but don't forget to tuck it back in.

Dear Zelda,

I am a small short-haired dog of indeterminate origin (a pound puppy). I've got a few tiny brown spots, but I'm mostly white all over. Every summer I like to lie in the sun, but I turn prematurely pink after a few minutes of exposure. Is there something I can do to avoid canine sunburn?

Please Don't Touch!

Dear Please Don't Touch,

I feel your pain. I learned the hard way. That's why I don't go anywhere in the dog days of summer without my shades and parasol!

Just because we're dogs doesn't mean we won't look like lobsters after a day in the sun. Dogs of any sort can get sunburned on their noses and in their ears. But shorthaired white dogs like you, whose tender skin is not fully covered by fur, really fry in the sun. Actually, any dog with white fur needs to watch the sun. Pink may be the "in" color this year, but pink skin is painful.

Remember that suntan lotion ad that showed the little dog yanking on the girl's swimsuit? He was saying, "Put some lotion on me, too!" Owners need to share the sunscreen (at least SPF 15) with their dogs, putting it on their noses, ears, and short white fur or exposed skin. Then you'll both sleep well at night.

Another summer tip is to always have plenty of cool, fresh drinking water available and *never* stay unattended in a closed car in the heat of the day. On those dog days of summer make sure you stay in the shade.

Zelda

Entrepreneurship

Being an entrepreneur is easier than spelling it.

Dear Zelda,

My sister and I (both in our forties and newly single parents) are trying to start a creative venture on our own. We have a couple of wonderful ideas but are having trouble implementing them. We saw your "mom" on *The Oprah Winfrey Show* and were totally inspired for the first time in a long time. We would love any guidance on how to get a new product off the ground, since our only experience is having babies! Is it totally hopeless, Zelda, or is there a road map out there somewhere? We are positive, creative, energetic women and want to make better lives for our children and ourselves. Please advise . . .

Raring to Go . . . but Don't Know Where to Start!

Dear Raring to Go,

Babies have been your business . . . now make business your baby. Women are starting businesses at twice the rate of men and expanding them twice as fast. That should make you feel hopeful, not hopeless. Read as much as you can about marketing a product or service. Two books were written for you: *Dive Right In—The Sharks Won't Bite: The Entrepreneurial Woman's Guide to Success* by Jane Wesman and *The Girl's Guide to Starting Your Own Business* by Caitlin Friedman and Kimberly Yorio. Along with very useful information like assessing finances, writing business plans, and hiring employees, they will tell you how to be a boss "without being a bitch."

Before you invest any money in your new business, seek advice from business owners in the industry. Carol researched the greeting card industry and then created something unique to the industry . . . me, a live dog with a real name and wisdom. Come up with an eye-catching name and logo (high school art students can be clever designers). Not always fun, but important, is to write a business plan that includes your financial and marketing/PR strategy. That will be your road map.

To register your business and apply for a federal Employer ID Number (EIN), call 1-800-TAX-FORM. If you need to get a copyright call the U.S. Copyright Office at 202-707-3000, or go online to www.copyright.gov. If your venture is in retail, you may need a state sales tax number. Check with your local city, county, and state to see what licenses you need, even if you're operating out of your garage. Get business cards, a CPA, and a lawyer who specializes in business. Save every receipt and vender bill and put your business name on everything. You should also network with your local women's business organizations.

There's a lot to do, but just take it in baby steps. From cradle to stroller to corporate office, this baby could be up and running before you know it.

Zelda

"Ex" Files

Give your "ex" a second chance . . . with someone else!

Dear Zelda,

I have been in a relationship with my girlfriend for about two years. I recently ran into my ex-girlfriend. She is now constantly e-mailing and calling me, trying desperately to get back together. I really love my current girlfriend but find myself drawn to my ex. What should I do?

Two Confused

Dear Two Confused,

Two years . . . two girls . . . to these two ears it sounds like it could be a little too much. To get to the square root of this byzantine relationship we're going to have to break it down to the sum of its parts: Is $X + U > Y + U$, or vice versa?

X = last girlfriend. She is X for a reason. Define X not by how fabulous she looks (or how great it is that she *now* laughs at all your jokes that she thought were "stupid" when you first dated), but by the variables that caused her to become X in the first place.

Y = current girlfriend. Y are you still with her? Because you love her and all the things that make her who she is? Or is it comfort (you can burp around her and she no longer yells "*Gross!*")? Or maybe because she pays her half of the rent?

U = Happy? Unhappy? Or just settling?

Study hard for this one, because it *is* a test. No slide rules, no calculators, and definitely no looking at your neighbor's paper. You have to figure this one out on your own by dividing, multiplying, subtracting, and adding memories and moments, both good and bad, to ensure that you have the right formula for an outstanding relationship with a common denominator. But before you go gallivanting off with an old flame, just remember that the food always smells better in another dog's bowl, that fantasy relationships with forbidden fruit are often just that—a fantasy, and that the reality may end up reminding you why you broke up in the first place. *Oh*, and the number-one test rule still applies: Anyone caught cheating gets an automatic *fail*.

Zelda

Family Matters

I don't suffer from insanity . . . I enjoy every minute of it.

Dear Zelda,

My teenage son is making me crazy . . . do they make Midol for boys? He has more mood swings than most pregnant women. I would say he is possessed, but nobody else would want to live with him in that body.

At the End of Her Rope Mom

Dear Mom,

Survival is hanging on after others let go. Mood swings, easy anger, and frustration are common during adolescence. Until his emotional swings subside, there are a few helpful things you can do for your son (short of exorcism) that will also ensure your own survival. Make sure he is getting enough rest (being tired can lead to sadness and irritability) and is getting regular exercise (being active produces endorphins that improve mood and control stress). Encourage him to put his thoughts down on paper, stay busy, and keep talking with you and his friends. He may tell you to go to hell, but open communication is important. I'm sure he knows just where your nuclear button is, but remain a patient, loving, supportive parent, and know where your nearest masseuse is.

Two great books I suggest are *Parent-Teen Breakthrough* by Mira Kirshenbaum and Charles Foster and *Get Out of My Life, but First Could You Drive Me and Cheryl to the Mall?* by Anthony Wolf. If your son's moods swing from feeling great to feeling suicidal, consult a mental health professional or call the National Suicide Prevention Hotline (1-800-SUICIDE). By the way, a new study has shown that asking teenagers about suicide won't make them more likely to contemplate it, as some parents fear. Since there is a strong genetic component involved, if there is a history of bipolar disorder in your family, it would be wise to talk to your doctor about the warning signs. At www.teengrowth.com, you can read answers to teenagers' questions regarding their mood swings.

While you're waiting for your son's hormones to stabilize, don't suffer from insanity . . . enjoy every minute of it. Keep smiling . . . learn to laugh . . . and *hang on*! You will both survive.

Zelda

Fathers

Dads rule by remote control.

Dear Zelda,

When my dad was in high school he played football, basketball, and baseball, and he was a star. My problem is that I'm not athletic, a fact he often points out to me in a negative way. When he introduces me he says, "This is my son. He's not an athlete, but he's smart." Then he laughs. This embarrasses me and makes me feel so bad that now I avoid him and close myself in my room when I come home from school. I want to please him but fear I will never be able to. Any ideas on how I can make him proud of me?

Not a Jock

Dear Not a Jock,

Your dad needs to get out of the clone zone. If he really wanted a Mini-Me he should have stayed in the laboratory with Dr. Frankenstein! People keep trying to clone animals. Can you blame them for wanting a world full of Zeldas? But your mom and dad brought you to life as a brand-new creation. You are your own person, with your own strengths and talents—even your own smile. You are an original.

Parents often project onto their children, wanting to see their offsping relive their own past glories while becoming "childaholics" in the process. They may be well meaning, but it is selfish. After all, it's your life, and it sounds to me like you've got your own glories ahead, but in the classroom, not on the playing field. I can relate. "Fetch" isn't even a game I can qualify for, let alone play. However I've found my own game . . . in front of a camera. Find something you're good at and go for it.

I also think it might be a good idea to talk with your mom about this. You need someone to go to bat for you. (That's language your dad will understand!) Ask her or a trusted adult friend to talk to your dad about your feelings. I hope that soon he'll be saying, "This is my son. He's terrific and smart and I couldn't be more proud!"

Zelda

Fear Factor

Facing your fear is easier than turning your back on it.

Dearest Zelda,

I really like this boy at school. There is a dance coming up and I want to ask him, but I am so nervous! What should I do?

Shy and Scared

Dear Shy and Scared,

Well, that is a tough one. It's scary to have feelings for someone and not know how they feel about you.

So what do I think you should do? Brush up on your dance moves! Don't let a little thing like fear stand in the way of boogyin' with your boy-to-be! Times have changed. Boys ask girls and girls ask boys. I'll bet some boys even expect it, and I can *guarantee* that most of them are just as scared to ask you. If you really like this boy, there's no better chance to let him know than asking him to a dance!

So just go on up and ask him. It's probably best to do it when your friends aren't around. That way there's no embarrassment for either one of you in front of other people, and it makes having a conversation a little easier without the peering eyes of . . . well . . . your peers. As embarrassing as this sounds, sometimes it's easiest to be straightforward and just say, "Hey, would you like to go to the dance with me?" Be strong, and be ready; the answer can go either way. He may already have a date, be busy that night, or . . . he just might say *yes*! But the really important thing is that you were brave enough to ask him, and I promise that you'll look back on that and be proud of yourself when you're older.

Whatever the answer, keep smiling. The main thing is the fact that you did it, and that, in itself, should have you dancin' in the hallways! Good luck!

Zelda

Fitness

Survival of the fittest!

Dear Zelda,

How do you maintain that girlish figure? I spend *minutes* on the treadmill and can't lose the potbelly. What do you advise?

EZ the Bulldog

Dear EZ,

A potbelly may be fine for swine, but you've got to lighten and tighten, and that means measuring the amount of dog food you consume every day. Ask your veterinarian how much food you need to keep fit for a dog your size and stick firmly to that amount. I go with one cup of lean, dry dog food in the morning and one cup in the evening. Believe me, I work hard for my 32-32-32 figure! I like to say, "If you want to stay svelte, tighten your belt . . . or maybe in our case, our collar." Don't make the mistake of buying a bigger collar because you are gaining weight. Cut back on your food consumption and keep the old collar. Look at it as a tape measure to keep pounds off hounds.

As for snacks, you may think that by begging for treats you will work up quite a sweat and burn calories, but don't overdo it. Remember, it's calories, calories, calories, and for most pups, people food just isn't what the doggy doctor ordered. If your owner can't resist giving you the occasional treat, suggest only healthy dog treats or veggies. Now, I beg for broccoli.

The real secret for maintaining my girlish figure, however, is that my owner likes to parade me around the neighborhood. She thinks it keeps the fat off both of us, and she's right. My suggestion is that you get your people to take you for more walks. To give them the hint, jump up and down excitedly by the door. That will burn off even more pounds! Just follow my advice and dieting will be made "EZ."

Zelda

Fit or Fat

On a scale from 1 to 10 . . . I'm a 15.

Dear Zelda,

Every time I look at one of your cards, I can relate. Zelda, we're not fat, we're fit. Like you, I was born big boned. What should I wear to make me look fit, not fat? I know that horizontal stripes are out, but do you have any other fashion suggestions?

Fellow Fit-Not-Fat Friend

Dear Fellow Fit-Not-Fat Friend,

You are correct, horizontal stripes are meant for three things: bumble bees, Easter eggs, and convicts (I assume you are none of these).

Your quest to be stylish and dress appropriately for your body type is admirable. With the current trends in fashion finally beginning to cater to us "bigger boned" gals, our options are becoming limitless. There's nothing wrong with giving those curves of yours an attractive and slimming bear hug . . . just make sure to keep them free of any eye-bulging (and flesh-bulging) death-grip clothes; they're soooooo not attractive.

Stick to one of the "Zelda Rules of Fashion": Make black, white, and tan your new best friends. Ideally you want harmony between you and your clothing, and trying to hide your frame inside a big floral muumuu (they are called that for a reason) will only bring chaos to your closet. Stand straight and tall, choosing clothes that "fit" with solid colors or tone-on-tones that contrast, resulting in flattering lines.

Match a dark skirt with a light-colored jacket, and add color around your face with a sassy silk scarf. Remember to "accentuate the positive." Big bust? How about a form-fitting single-breasted jacket or shirt that shows a little skin and says that you're proud of what your mama gave ya? Large behind? Flaunt it, girl. If it's workin' for J-Lo, it can work for us, too. Pick a pant that's fitted at the hips and waist, but flares just a bit at the bottom. Leave the big floral prints, stripes, and polka dots for . . . who am I kidding, no one should wear those! Anyway, if it's question-a-bull, don't make the mistake of thinking you can get away with it "just this once." You can't.

Following a few of these basic rules of dress will transform your wardrobe from "frumpy faux paws" to "flawlessly fit and fabulous" in no time.

Zelda

Friendship

Jewelry is precious, but friendship is priceless.

Dear Zelda,

Do you agree that diamonds are
a girl's best friend?

Curious

Dear Curious,

A gem of a friend trumps a diamond any day. In spite of all their facets, diamonds can't offer you advice, lend you a hand, share a good story, or bring soup when you're sick. They can't laugh with you, philosophize with you, reminisce with you, or tell you there's spinach caught in your teeth. Like a dog or a teddy bear, good friends always listen. You might keep a diamond on your finger, but you keep a friend in your heart. Just give me a zirconia-studded collar and *zuper* friends like Zoe and ZeeZee, and I'll pass up a trip to Tiffany & Co. any day. I don't weigh my wealth by carats, but by caring friends.

Zelda

P.S. If I remember correctly, "Diamonds Are a Girl's Best Friend" was the theme song from the 1953 movie *Gentlemen Prefer Bulldogs* . . . or was it "*Blondes*"?

Giving Back

Give someone a hand.

Dear Zelda,

My dog, Gracie, is the sweetest thing you can imagine. I read in *Ladies' Home Journal* that you work with children who have learning disabilities. Can you tell me what you do and how you got started? I'd love to share my Gracie with children and maybe we could help them learn to read, too.

Well-Read

Dear Well-Read,

Gracie certainly may be sweet, but, girl, you don't sound like such a bad sugar substitute yourself. It's very sweet of you (and Gracie) to want to help those children who may need it. Who doesn't love a cuddly, slobber-kissin', love-a-bull dog?

You are correct—I do work with children through a wonderful international organization called the Delta Society. It's dedicated to promoting the power of animals to alleviate human suffering. They were kind enough to take this old dog and train and certify me as an official "Delta Society therapy dog," and it's one of my proudest achievements.

My suggestion to you is to start with baby steps and look at programs close to your area. Dog therapy groups are popping up all over the country. Children love being able to read and interact with us furry friends because we don't judge or laugh when mistakes are made or when words aren't pronounced quite right or even if takes a while to finish a sentence. Our attention and affection come unconditionally, and we expect nothing in return but the occasional pat on the head or scratch on the belly (a personal favorite . . . especially as mine is getting bigger!).

Giving a child the opportunity to read without all the judgments or expectations that human beings tend to bring with them can help to break down walls and allow the child to actually pay attention and *learn*. Here is some contact information that can help you find opportunities in your area: Delta Society, www.deltasociety.org; Intermountain Therapy Animals, www.therapyanimals.org or 801-272-3439. Also check out the Reading Education Assistance Dogs (R.E.A.D.) program, whose mission it is to improve the literacy skills of children through the assistance of registered Pet Partner therapy teams. Today's baby steps in education are tomorrow's giant leaps for our children!

Zelda

Graduation

What do you want out of graduation . . . ? Out!

Dear Zelda,

My two pugs, Lexie and Wesley, just graduated from obedience school, and I want to have a party for them. Can you give me any suggestions to make their graduation party a success? I'm inviting friends with two and four legs.

Owner of Pets with Degrees

Dear Owner of Pets with Degrees,

Let's party! You came to the right place if you're looking for the ultimate party animal. Give me the chance, and I'll celebrate just about anything. I have a few simple suggestions for organizing the perfectly planned pug party:

First is location, location, location. If your backyard is too small or you don't have one, look into renting space at a doggy day care center or training facility. You might even plan to have your party at a public park if there aren't regulations against it.

Next, send out fun invitations to guests who have dogs that get along well with Lexie and Wesley. Try making your own graduation-themed cards: Lexie and Wesley in caps and gowns always works, or you could send out miniature diplomas in the shape of dog bones. Make sure to mention that this is a party to celebrate your dogs' "Pet Degrees," and that you are very proud of their big accomplishment!

Third, plan the food. There are some paws-itively delicious canine cakes available in the *Three Dog Bakery Cookbook* by Dan Dye and Mark Beckloff. My favorite is the "Let 'Em Eat Cake." There is also a recipe for "Graduation Good Dog Goodies" that will have your pugs and their pals munching and crunching and woofing them down.

Finally, what would a party be without games? I suggest you avoid dominance-provoking games like tug-of-war (unfortunately a favorite game of mine), and go for games like Frisbee and fetch. You could also hold a talent show. Have each dog/owner show off his/her trick, and let the owner explain how their dog learned to do it. You might even let the owners compete with tricks of their own! You can find descriptions of party games in *Beyond Fetch: Fun Interactive Activities for You and Your Dog*, by D. Caroline Coile, Ph.D.

Congratulations to Lexie and Wesley for their "Wagna" Cum Laude pet degrees. Have fun and be creative at your party, and remember, the success is in de-tails!

Zelda

Hair

Even goddesses have bad-hair days.

Dear Zelda,

Every time I look in the mirror I see more gray hairs. Many of my friends have their hair colored to hide the gray. Should I succumb and let my hair go gray or should I stay the brunette that I've always been? By the way, I'm forty-seven years old and don't feel ready to resemble my gray-haired granny.

Born a Brunette

Dear Born a Brunette,

Go back to your roots! Your brunette roots, that is. Some people may say you look just fine as a granny wannabe, but what counts is how you feel. You'll feel more youthful, attractive, and confident when you're not worried that you appear to be much older than you really are. You can color your hair yourself or have it done professionally. Either way, you can choose to use a hair dye with natural ingredients if you're sensitive to chemicals. Me? I'd go with the best professional around. Have fun with it. By adding highlights to your hair you may also be adding some highlights to your life. When in doubt, think of the late Julia Child. She dyed her hair red to the very end of her ninety-one years. No one ever called the feisty chef "Granny"! It's AARF, not AARP.

Zelda

Heartbreak

Only love can mend a broken heart . . .

Dear Zelda,

My boyfriend and I had been dating for two years when, out of nowhere, he broke up with me. He claimed I was not "the one." I, on the other hand, thought he was "the one." I never want to feel like this again. How do I get over this and move on with my life?

Heartbroken

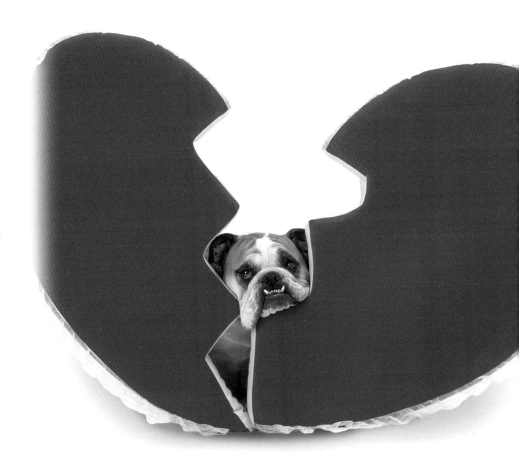

Dear Heartbroken,

There's a song by Three Dog Night that's been around for years called "One." It's a true American classic (by an incred-i-bully well-named band). One of the lyrics in the song states, "One is the loneliest number." Ironic, isn't it? It's the loneliest number, yet we use it to describe the "one" person in this vast universe who makes us feel completely "unlonely."

Now, the reality here is that in order to get over "the one," you need to feel comfortable with the real "one": yourself. So many times we can get stuck in the rut of being "two," forgetting that it took two "ones" to make you the great "two" you once were. Yeah, he was great and wonderful. Unfortunately, he's gone and you feel like a big chunk of your strength and independence went with him.

The times they are a changin' and you need to grasp your new freedom and ride like the wind. Take this time to get back to your own roots. You don't need another man to unbreak your heart; you need to get back to being comfortable with yourself and convince yourself that you are smart, sassy, and, yes, single. No matter how great the two of you were together, you have your own independent identity, and it's that identity that you need to nurture now. It's this song of confidence and your devil-may-care attitude that will show the "we" of the world your independent, imaginative, impossibly impressive "me" of the world.

Before you know it, you'll be giving a cheeky smile to some handsome passerby while sitting in Starbucks with your tall, half-caf, sugar-free vanilla latte, reading the latest *Cosmo* and wondering if that short skirt that's hot for fall was meant to reside in your lineup this season. It's all about not being afraid to be a strong, independent "one" for a while, because sometimes being a good "one" is a heck of a lot better than being part of a bad "two."

Focus, girlfriend . . . there's a new "one" on your horizon, and that one is YOU.

Zelda

Here Comes Summer

Thongs on my feet beat a thong on my seat.

Dear Zelda,

For over sixteen years, I have worked as a secretary for an oil and gas company. In the past two years, I have not been able to relax and totally enjoy myself on vacation because all I think about is work and all of the e-mails and typing that will be waiting for me when I get back. What advice can you give to an overworked, stressed-out, burned-out middle-aged woman?

Stressed Out in Texas

P.S. The last time I took a vacation was one year ago!

Dear Stressed Out in Texas,

As I always say, "Let your vocation be your vacation." That doesn't mean every day at work has to be a picnic . . . we can't all be teaching pilates in the South Pacific, and last time I checked, there aren't a lot of high-paying jobs out there in the field of massage receiving. Even so, there should be some aspects of your job that leave you a little more than just "overworked, stressed-out, and burned out." Not only is your vocation no vacation, but now your vacations are actually being ruined by your vocation! Your brain is telling you something very simple . . . something needs to change.

It sounds like you're a perfectionist and a people pleaser, and for that, you pay a heavy price. Every day is a gift we are lucky to receive, but you don't even have time to unwrap the present! It's time to put some balance in your work-a-day world. Short of quitting, the first thing you should change is your attitude. Obviously you are good at what you do . . . probably too good. Why don't you try being a little bit bad every now and then? You don't *have* to finish that pile of typing today; after all, it's past 5:00. There are times when you need to learn to just say "no."

Start by not being so perfect. Either delegate to someone else or admit to your boss that there just aren't enough hours in the day to answer all the e-mails, finish all the typing, and maintain your mental stability. Let your boss solve it or hire someone to help. You've worked for this company for sixteen years; most marriages don't last that long these days. You are incredibly valuable to them, and it's totally reasonable to let them know that you need some changes to keep you happy and healthy.

If they're unwilling to compromise, look for a job that *will* make you happy. There are so many companies that would love to have someone with your character and experience. Time is the ultimate nonrenewable resource. Don't waste yours. Who knows, with some luck maybe this time next year you'll be able to take that vacation and even enjoy it.

Zelda

Men

Wanted: Man with fire

Dear Zelda,

Where have all the men gone? The Clark Gable, Cary Grant types who swept women off their feet. I'm in my thirties, single and still looking for the man who will make me swoon. I watch old movies and wonder what happened to the men who brought women flowers and chocolates. Where are the men who would write poetry as well as protect you? All I see are guys drinking beer, playing video games, and acting like children. What's up with men today?

Wanted: Clones for Clark and Cary

Dear Wanted: Clones,

Personally, I have always been a Bogart girl, but then I do have a thing for jowls.

Regardless of your classic-film crush, whether it was Clark Gable courting Vivien Leigh in *Gone with the Wind* or Cary Grant being cavalier with Audrey Hepburn in *Charade*, the stereotypes for men were very different in those days. But to be fair, it isn't just male stereotypes that have changed; look at us women. While we've been busy burning our bras, starting our own companies, and generally saving the world, there are probably men out there still longing for June Cleaver clones. That doesn't mean I'm going to put on an apron tonight and make meatloaf, but I would say that modern gender roles are confusing for a lot of people, myself included.

It sounds like you are looking for an old-fashioned guy. The answer to your predicament boils down to one word: communication. I've often seen people walk away from a problem without discussing it with the other person. How many relationships have you lost that could have been saved if you'd just let the man know that it is important to you that he opens the door or brings you flowers? Women *and* men need to communicate better today.

The next time you meet a man who interests you, tell him what you're looking for. Let him know that gardenias are your favorite flower, and that nothing makes you happier than a box of Moonstruck chocolates. I bet he'll get the picture, and soon you'll be flush with flowers and swooning over the way he treats you. If not, have the resolve to move on to the next audition, and hold another casting call for a Clark or a Cary. Be persistent, look in the right places, be honest and respectful in your communication, and you'll find him.

Zelda

Honesty

You can't always blame the dog!

Dear Zelda,

A few months ago I tried computer dating. After looking at the men who were listed, I decided to "fudge" a little on my age. It seemed that all the men my age were looking for younger women so I just subtracted ten years from my "true" age. Now I'm in a pickle because I met someone I really like and he keeps referring to me as his "younger woman." Help me, Zelda.

In a Pickle

Dear In a Pickle,

Fibbing about one or two years is definitely "fudging" a little . . . fibbing about being *ten* years younger is a whole big pan of "fudge"! It's a regular fudge cake! But let me just say . . . *you go, girl* for being able to pull it off! I'd need five quarts of BOTOX and a small detachment from the Army Corps of Engineers to manage that.

    Anyone who plays the Internet dating game knows it requires a certain amount of anonymity to avoid the three S's: spam, stalkers, and psychos (hey . . . no one said I was a spelling bee champion). It's impossible to miss the faint hum of "little white lies" taking flight from countless keyboards. What most Internet daters forget is that this is the *perfect* opportunity for you to be completely honest about yourself and what you're looking for, because you don't have to face the prospect of a harsh face-to-face rejection. It's a great way to let possible suitors read your profile and decide from there whether a conversation should ensue, and a great way for you to do the same.

    I understand the temptation to fudge, especially when you feel you are missing out on the legions of eligible bachelors who screen out people of a certain age. The problem is your plan actually worked! Now you're stuck with the reality that you may have nabbed a catch who, in turn, thinks he caught something else. Unfortunately, your "fudge" is about to reach its expiration date. He'll find out sometime, and hearing it from you, in all your youthful glow, will hopefully help to soften the blow.

    Be honest *now*, because if this relationship has any chance, he'll need to know, and the sooner the better. If he's been online dating for a while he may give you a little slack, but no one likes to be deceived. I've said it before and I'll say it again, "A relationship is built on a solid foundation of trust." No, really, it is.

    We're all wishing for the best, but in the future, you may want to put your online dating on a fudge-free diet . . . or at least cut the recipe in half.

Zelda

Houseguests

Houseguests from hell? Can we send them home?

Dear Zelda,

A couple of weeks ago my best friend asked if I could dog-sit her three dogs while she went to visit her parents in upstate New York. The dogs, while very lovable, scratched my doors and chewed a hole in my new couch. The dogs are home with their owner now, but I'm stuck with the damage. Should I just pay for the repairs, or should I ask her to take care of the things they destroyed?

Three Dog Night-mare

Dear Three Dog Night-mare,

It sounds like you've been the victim of some extremely hazardous houseguest hounds! Your wards seemed to think that "sofa" was an item on their menu, and that perhaps an open-door policy just meant they got to tunnel their way through the front door. We all like to be accommodating, but in this case it's definitely not unreasonable to ask your best friend to take care of the damage or at least help with repairs. This isn't the easiest topic to broach, however, so you need to be careful that your friendship isn't endangered.

Before you confront her, make a list of the damages and get an estimate for repairs. Invite her over for a cool glass of whatever and tell her you'd like to talk about the dogs. Once she's there, show her the damage done by her playful pooches. When she sees the hole in your new couch, she should say something like, "Ouch! I'll take care of this." Same for the doors. If you feel awkward, don't worry . . . everyone feels awkward in these situations.

Personally, I would suggest allowing her to pay part of the costs and you pay the rest yourself, in the spirit of goodwill and to honor your friendship. At the end of the day, you have to ask yourself whether this is going to negatively impact your friendship, and if so, whether it is worth it. Only you will be able to weigh these big decisions, but keep in mind that a good friend is more valuable than any door or sofa. That said, in order for your friendship to remain healthy, *you* need to feel that you can honestly express your feelings and frustrations, even when they involve your friend herself, or her pooches.

Unfortunately friendships are often soured or severed because of situations like this. Don't let it happen to you. Be open about your concerns, but also let her know that your friendship is by far the most important thing. With any luck, you'll have the house all repaired and ready just about the time she decides to take another road trip!

Zelda

Household Hints

Cleaning . . . it's a good thing.

Dear Zelda,

Our cleaning service isn't helping clean very much, and we never have very much time to clean ourselves. Do you have any tips on how to clean more quickly?

Dirty Girl

Dear Dirty Girl,

Even good girls get dirty sometimes, and so do our homes. Never fear, your domestic diva dog is here to help. Actually, my only domestic quality is that I live in a house. But I'm a good listener, and I've picked up several cleaning hints over the years . . . like just turn down the lights. No, seriously, I do have some suggestions to help you clean up your act.

It helps to be organized, and it helps even more if you start with a to-do list. You can also plan the order of operations so you don't end up, say, sweeping the floor before you dust the furniture. Start with the first job on your list and do one thing at a time, crossing off each task as you complete it. Set a timer for each job, and when it goes off you should plan to be finished. This helps eliminate distractions like answering the telephone (let voice mail field your calls), spending a lot of extra time sweeping in front of the television while your favorite show is on, or turning your clothes folding into a private fashion show. Focus on getting the job done.

For all this organization and efficiency, you shouldn't try to be a "Supergirl." You can, and should, delegate some of the tasks to others in the house and get rid of the "I can only do it myself" responsibility. You aren't the only one who knows how to fold laundry or do dishes. Sure, vacuuming sucks, so share the job with someone.

Finally, if your home reaches disaster proportions and you are stressed by the mess, take time to clear the clutter. No one can clean quickly when surrounded by clutter. When in doubt, throw it out! Work ahead, not behind, and concentrate your time where it counts.

Being productive every day doesn't come from working harder but working smarter. You won't end up dog-tired, and you'll still have time afterward for a catnap.

Zelda

Insecurities

Born to be mild

Dear Zelda,

A few months ago I heard your owner speak to a large group of executive women. She was so calm, and public speaking seemed to be effortless for her. I am a young attorney working for a good law firm, but every time I have to speak to a group I am filled with anxiety. Do you have any tips to help me overcome my fear of public speaking? I literally can't sleep the night before I have to make a presentation, and my hands shake when I'm in front of a crowd.

Powerless at the Podium

Dear Powerless at the Podium,

I wouldn't say that you are powerless . . . I'd just say that you haven't harnessed your power and pointed it in the right direction. But be comforted by the knowledge that fear of public performance is incredibly common. Did you know that Barbra Streisand avoided performing in public for nearly twenty years because of stage fright? Indeed, it is the fear of looking foolish that ends up making us look foolish.

Most of us are consumed by the pursuit of perfection, and the fear of failure in front of an audience is all the more frightening. Wow, so many witnesses to our imperfections! Step one in losing the butterflies is to let go of a bit of that perfectionism, relax, and realize that everyone listening knows you are just human. It's perfectly okay to be nervous—most people are—but don't let worrying about it take over your entire presentation.

Step two is to be prepared. Be sure that you know exactly what you'll say, where you'll say it, what kind of connection your laptop uses, and all the other nasty little details. This doesn't mean every last thing has to be perfect. It won't be. But the better you know your presentation, the less you will have to worry about remembering what comes next or panicking at the last minute because your slides aren't showing up on the screen. Write your presentation down on note cards that are set for each part of your speech. Consulting notes is not uncommon, and in the case of an emergency, like forgetting your next line, you'll simply look . . . prepared.

Step three is practice, practice, practice. Practice in front of the mirror, practice in front of a friend, and if you have the chance, practice in the room where you will be speaking. Someone once asked my owner, "What makes a good speaker?" Her reply was "Five hundred speeches." With every talk you give to an audience you will become more confident and comfort-a-bull. You've got the power, now go out and use it!

Zelda

In the Stink

Excuse me? I don't think so!

Dear Zelda,

Everyone in my office is reading *Dear Zelda* and we love your straightforward, somewhat out-of-the-box advice. One of our coworkers here at our brokerage firm has really bad body odor. Several of us have discussed it and don't know how to let him know that he'd probably have more friends if he could do something about his scent. How do we go about telling him without hurting his feelings?

In the Stink

Dear In the Stink,

I'm all about being "au natural," but please . . . in a brokerage firm?
Fuhgedaboudit. Body odor for me is like one of those colored hair scrunchies
women wear—they both can be worn only when doing laundry in the privacy
of your own home. Yet your coworker has decided to air his dirty laundry in a
place where clean power suits mingle with tidy power lunches. *Un-accept-a-bull!*
I say bring your laundry basket of complaints to him for his sake and yours.
You probably want to avoid using phrases like "PU" and *"What the heck stinks
around here?"* But at the same time, you want to let him know that you are
concerned not only for his health but for his career. Make sure to pick a place of complete privacy
(with an incredible ventilation system), and choose either you or someone he trusts to talk with
him about it. If he truly sees your concern, and the fact that you're not being judgmental, you may
find him receptive to your laundry list of woes.

  Do be prepared, though, that there could be a medical reason why he isn't able to wear
deodorant. Many people are either allergic to deodorants or have a chemical imbalance resulting
from an enzyme deficiency that goes beyond proper hygiene. At the very least you will clean up
your concerns and leave the rest for him to fold and sort.

Zelda

Jobs

It's a dog-eat-dog world.

Dear Zelda,

For the first time in more than twenty years I'm out pounding the pavement looking for work. I won't bore you with the details about the "you-know-what" in my office who turned my boss against me. I'll just say she's a "female dog," and it rhymes with "itch." I don't think you can tell me anything useful. The plain fact is nobody wants to hire me. With my luck, I'll be a homeless bag lady by the end of the month.

Over the Hill

Dear Over the Hill,

What you've got to get over is your bad attitude. You're having a nonstop pity party, blaming everyone else but yourself for your current situation. And by the way, if the colleague who pushed you aside is as awful as you say, the woman is definitely un-dog-like! (We rhymes-with-itch-es need to stick together!)

My advice is to turn your frown upside down. Start smiling at everybody. Smile at yourself in the mirror. When I do that it kind of perks up my jowls and makes me smile even bigger. Then, after you've improved your attitude, why don't you update your look? Pick out stylin' new eyeglass frames. Get a hip new hairdo and jazz up your wardrobe. You'll look better and feel better about yourself.

Next up is your résumé. Make sure it reflects your accomplishments and the contributions you made to your last company's success. Don't hold back from bragging on yourself. Then, when you go for interviews, let that can-do attitude shine through. Employers look for something called "fire in the belly." Unfortunately, it has nothing to do with spicy Thai food, which I love. What it means is passion, enthusiasm, and lots of energy. Show that you've got it and a great new job will be yours. Just remember to treat your new coworkers right, no matter if you're "itching" to do otherwise.

Zelda

Losing

Learning how to lose is half the game.

Dear Zelda,

Last month I was selected as employee of the month by the big retail company where I work. The problem I'm having is that the other two employees who were nominated have turned against me and are saying negative things about me. When I was selected as employee of the month I felt like a winner and was proud and happy. Now I'm feeling like the real loser. Any advice?

Winner or Loser?

Dear Winner or Loser?

There is no question that you're a winner; clearly you're the best in show all the way around. But as you have learned, every win comes with its share of loss. Here, the problem isn't you; it's the two other employees. No one likes to lose, and being a good loser takes character, which is something your coworkers seem to lack. But you know what takes even more character than being a good loser? Being a good winner.

Being a good winner means not just being humble and gracious in victory, but also being forgiving to those who are jealous of your success. That doesn't mean you should just accept your coworkers' bad behavior and silently take their abuse, but it does mean understanding why they might be jealous of you in the first place . . . after all, they've got a lot to be jealous of! Keep doing that fabulous work on the job and be professional in the workplace, even when dealing with your sniping coworkers.

If it becomes a problem, talk to them. Sometimes all it takes is confronting the issue directly to clear the air and move on. If that doesn't work, then talk to your boss. You may lose those coworkers as friends, but with those kind of friends, who needs enemies?

In John McCain's recent book *Character Is Destiny*, he talks about how many of our heroes had to lose before they won. Think Gandhi, Abraham Lincoln, or Nelson Mandela. They all had to do what they thought was right, and these heroes all lost many times, but when they lost, they learned from it, they stuck to their beliefs, and they moved on to win. It sounds like you've done your share of both winning and losing in this past month, and now it's time to learn from the experience, grow beyond it, and come out happy, healthy, loving your job, and still radiating that employee-of-the-month glow. Go get 'em!

Zelda

Midlife Crisis

Currently in training for a midlife crisis

Dear Zelda,

I need some help. I am a middle-aged married woman, but I have a next-door neighbor who keeps suggesting that we "get together." He's my age and has a wife of his own. How do I discourage him without ruining our neighborly friendship?

Just Neighborly

Dear Just Neighborly,

I wouldn't stress about your neighbor unless Fred Affair starts tapping on your bedroom window some night. Until then, tweak his suggestion and plan a spouses-included get-together. If he keeps two-stepping toward you, tell him to go dance to a different tune on a different block. Your neighborliness doesn't include any over-the-fence fling. If he still doesn't listen, you might need to hose him down with some cold water.

Zelda

Mothers

Every mother is a Queen Mother.

Dear Zelda,

My mom wants to become a drummer in a rock band, and I don't think it's right at her age (forties). She has always loved beating on things—not me thankfully, but pots and pans, tables, doors, etc. She has been a single mom for ten years and bought a set of drums about five years ago. She's actually pretty good, but I can't imagine what my friends will think when I tell them my mom is playing the drums with a group of long-haired guys at a local bar. How can I convince her to drop the drum idea?

Missing a Beat

Dear Missing a Beat,

Hey, go Mom! Our applause to anyone who discovers a passion in their life, and it sounds as if your mother has. Being a drummer in a rock band obviously isn't the image you have for your mother, but maybe she is ready to move on to another identity. Just remember how you felt when Mom was calling the shots for you: hair judgments, Mom's version of "hip" clothes . . . and what about those grades?

Sometimes the closer you are to someone the more critical you can be. Imagine what my owner's son thought when she told him she was starting a greeting card company by dressing up her dog! So get outside of yourself. Think about what will make Mom happy, and be happy for her. The best gift you could give her is your unconditional and loving support as she pursues her dream. You might even drum up some business for her band.

In life we can all lighten up a little where our families and friends are concerned. It's a good thing to march to the beat of a different drummer. So what if the drummer just happens to be your mom?

Zelda

Mothers-in-Law

If it's not one thing, it's your mother.

Dear Zelda,

I have tried to be warm to my mother-in-law, but I find her insensitive much of the time. She has mastered the art of guilt and will sometimes say uncensored thoughts that hurt our feelings—especially my teenage daughter's. And, she seems to care more about her animals than her family. I don't want to speak badly of her in front of my children, but sometimes it's very difficult. How do I include her in family gatherings without feeling the stress of her presence?

Stressed Out

Dear Stressed Out,

Isn't it amazing that in the *huge* boxing ring of relationships you can be related to someone . . . yet not relate?

People like your mother-in-law relate to one thing and one thing only—confrontation. They are used to saying what they want without consequence. I think it's time to implement what I call a "Confrontation TKO." Don't worry, no one is physically harmed in this ring of emotions, but there may be a nice sucker punch to a certain someone's ego. This is the training plan: The next time you feel one of her insensitive punches heading your way, slap on the mental boxing gloves and give her the ol' one-two combo with a simple phrase and follow-up that I think you'll find very effective. No matter where you both are, no matter who's standing around, look her straight in the eyes, mental boxing gloves to the ready, feet standing firm, with a voice as strong as Muhammad Ali, and say, "Why would you say that to me?"

This next part is very important. Don't back down your stare and don't walk away. She will not expect it, but trust me, she will feel it. If you can wait for the answer I think you'll find that you've thrown her off balance, and by a unanimous decision . . . round one will go to the new champ formerly known as "Stressed Out." This may sound simple but when you say it with enough conviction, you will be dancing around like a featherweight champ, floatin' like a butterfly and stingin' like a bee.

Now, as for caring more about her animals . . . can people ever give animals enough love? I may be biased . . . but I say not. Good luck, champ!

Zelda

Nuptial Nightmares

Love forever. Easy? Never.

Dear Zelda,

I have a lot of anxieties about my wedding day, but I'm really uneasy about my fiancé wanting to have Speedo (a lab-greyhound mix) be his best man, or rather "best dog." Speedo's great, but it doesn't seem right to have him be part of such a formal and special religious ceremony. Needless to say, I didn't laugh when my fiancé said Speedo is ecumenically minded and will fit right in. I have nightmares about him lifting his leg on all the flowers or something worse. Help!

Bummed Bride

Dear Bummed Bride,

If a maid of honor can be a man, then the best man can certainly be a dog. Everyone knows a dog is man's best friend. Andy Rooney says, "The average dog is a nicer person than the average person." I'll wag to that. My philosophy is: Why be ordinary and have a cookie-cutter ceremony? The image of Speedo sporting a tie, vest, and cummerbund to match your fiancé's attire . . . now that's fetching and unique. Speedo could be the "new" in "something old, something new, something borrowed, something blue." Just don't you be the "blue."

The best man offers moral support, stands next to the groom during the processional, walks with the maid of honor in the recessional, and mingles with the guests at the reception. A dog can do all this. So what if he can't host the bachelor party, embarrass you during the first toast at the reception, or spill the beans if your groom gets cold feet? That's what a second groomsman is for. Who knows, your fiancé might compromise and settle for Speedo being the guest book attendant or ring bearer. Those would still be positions of honor, albeit less conspicuous. If he's going to be present, Speedo might as well do something significant, even if he "I doo-doos" somewhere in the process. (You might consider having an outside wedding, by the way.) We canines can handle more than table-scrap patrol. You and your fiancé need to tango on this issue, not tangle. For avoiding anxiety-inducing snafus, refer to *The Complete Guide for the Anxious Bride: How to Avoid Everything That Could Go Wrong on Your Big Day* by Leah Ingram.

Speedo is important to your fiancé and is going to be part of your life. I say let him be part of your wedding. It's the off-beat, comical accents in your wedding that will snap your garter every time you reminisce.

Zelda

Parenting

Enough about me . . . where did your parents go wrong?

Dear Zelda,

I am a single mom, and my teenage daughter and I just got into an awful fight. I kicked her out of the house and told her not to return until she was ready to change her ways (like keeping her room clean) and to apologize for the names she called me. She is staying with a girlfriend's family so I know she is safe and not on the streets. Was I wrong to kick her out? How can I get my daughter back without losing face?

Mom in Need

Dear Mom in Need,

Being a single mom (or dad) is one of the toughest jobs anyone can have. Not only are you responsible for your own well-being, but you're responsible for the well-being of another person. If that person is a teenager, they're also probably making some bad decisions that *you* have to live with. This isn't a problem of losing face . . . it's a problem of potentially losing a daughter. Just because you know where she is right now doesn't guarantee you'll know tomorrow. Millions of children run away each year, and where they go and what they go through can be a far worse nightmare than name calling and bad room cleaning.

I'm all about tough love, especially if the punishment fits the crime, but go get your daughter. If it's really just about the room cleaning and name calling, the punishment sounds like it may have gotten out of hand in the heat of the moment. You don't want one bad argument to end up being a lifelong regret. You both have had time to simmer down, and it's probably a good time to have a long talk about the difficulties of your relationship.

Make sure she knows that, no matter what, you love her more than anything in the world. As hard as it is, especially when you are angry and things are tense, the most important part of working through problems is listening. It's the key to unlocking a better understanding of the other person and being able to process the situation rationally before heated feelings become drastic measures.

If it's beyond the point of a good heart-to-heart, then maybe it's time for family counseling. Sometimes it's good to have a "professional" sit in and help you talk through things. You're a great mom for writing in, and your love and concern for your daughter is evident. But no matter how much you disagree or how angry you get, unless she is seriously breaking the law or endangering you or your family, your home should always be open to her. It's one of the most important things we do as family.

We're sending good thoughts along with licks and wags to both of you.

Zelda

Peer Pressure

Peer pressure is really fear pressure.

Dear Zelda,

I'm sixteen and just got my driver's license. My problem is my friends who think driving fast and crazy is cool. Do you have any suggestions for getting them to drive more responsibly?

Drivin' Me Crazy

Dear Drivin' Me Crazy,

Way to go! You are now officially a "responsible driver," and thousands of drivers, every day, depend on you to be just that. We view cars as the quickest way to get from point A to point B, but we forget that a car is the deadliest weapon most of us will ever control. Driving is a privilege, and the fact that you've taken the time to write this letter shows that you understand this privilege and the responsibility that goes with it.

As for your friends, I can think of a few things you might say to help cool down their need for speed. Let them know that in the world of insurance rates, a sixteen-year-old is the most expensive driver in the nation (in some cases *ten times* more expensive than drivers between the ages of thirty and fifty-nine). These high rates mean that sixteen-year-olds are also the most likely to wreck or get killed in a car, precisely because they drive too fast and don't know their limits. Any tickets or accidents during this time can double and even triple your rate.

You might also let them know that teen drivers have the highest rate of out-of-control, single-car crashes in which speeding is the culprit, and fatal accidents are more likely to occur when you're with friends. Too much talking (and hormones and peer pressure) leads to distraction, which can lead to accidents, severe injury, and ultimately . . . death. It sounds gruesome, but two out of three teens who die in automobile accidents are the *passengers*. Tell your friends that even if they want to take risks with their own lives, they should have a little more respect for the lives of their friends and everyone else on the road.

At your age, wisdom may fall on deaf ears. The best thing you can do is try to keep your friends safe, set a good example, and when you're a passenger in someone else's car and they are being unsafe, don't be afraid to ask them to stop and let you out. It may not sound very cool, but trust me, getting hurt or killed in an accident, when you had your whole life ahead of you, is much less cool.

Zelda

Pet Peeves

If swimming is good for your figure . . . explain whales!

Dear Zelda,

My husband thinks he's being helpful, but I think he's being hurtful. Ever since I had our first child he's been hinting that I should start to work out. I'm not the workout type and he knows it. He's always throwing out "ideas" for options: swimming, walking, tennis. I do want to lose a few of my "new mommy pounds," but his "helpful hints" are making me less interested in doing so. I wish he'd take five and let me handle it when I'm ready.

Baby Fat

Dear Baby Fat,

Congratulations on the new arrival! Wouldn't it be fabulous if we women were *only* responsible for carrying, birthing, and nurturing our bouncing little bundles of joy, while our poor, exhausted husbands took over the arduous task of losing "just a few extra pounds" for us? Yeah . . . when bulldogs fly!

I'm sure he has your best interests at heart, but it can come off sounding insensitive and even a little selfish when his not-so-subtle hints become a constant reminder that you have yet one more thing to do. As if sleepless nights, endless feedings, and those oh-so-cute poopy diapers aren't enough to push you over the edge.

Baby fat? Darn right it is. It's something that every mother gets to wear proudly, symbolizing both the "new arrival" and the long journey ahead. You're no different than any other mother who's given birth, and all you need is a little time to let your body return to normal. Make things simple on yourself and "exercise" your right to be a new mother. Tell your husband you appreciate his help, but you'll ask for it when you need it. And right now, you don't need it. It really is that simple!

If you would like to become a little more active without feeling like you're caving in to his pressure, try to find something the two of you could do together a few times a week, like taking the baby out for walks around the neighborhood. If nothing else, you'll find out how good he is at taking his own suggestions!

Be proud of all you've accomplished this far, Mom! And tell your husband that if he's really excited about exercise, you know a certain bulldog who has been looking for someone to carry her from her bed to the kitchen and back three times a day.

Zelda

Petty Things

Don't sweat the petty things, and don't pet the sweaty things.

Dear Zelda,

I have a new boyfriend and my dog, Brutus, starts barking whenever my boyfriend kisses me. This doesn't seem like a big deal, but it's starting to get annoying. It may sound "petty," but it is bothering us. Zelda, how can I stop his bad habit?

Smoocher

Dear Smoocher,

It sounds like Brutus is just being protective, and he may not understand what your boyfriend is doing when he moves in for a smooch. You could always try to convince your boyfriend to sit down with Brutus and explain the facts of life, or more realistically, get your boyfriend to just spend some one-on-one time playing with Brutus. As long as your boyfriend remains a stranger to him, Brutus is going to be suspicious; the more time they spend together, the more comfortable Brutus will be and the less likely he'll be to regard your boyfriend as a threat and raise a ruckus.

Another, more immediate solution (while Brutus is still getting used to the new guy) is to just keep Brutus occupied with something he likes. Keep *him* busy, and you and your boyfriend can get . . . ah, well . . . busy. While your first instinct may be to put Brutus in another room to keep him quiet, this may or may not actually work, and it will definitely make him associate your boyfriend's visits with getting locked up . . . not exactly the best way to make him take a liking to your new beau. Instead, just get him a toy that will keep him chewing for a long time.

Start by checking out your local pet store; we particularly like the Kong brand dog toys and snacks. I'm partial to the Kong Jawrobics Dog Toy (try that one five times fast). Kongs can be filled and refilled with peanut butter, soft cheese, treats, or Kong filler. We always have a few of them on hand (we fill up the extras and keep them in the freezer), and it's good to have them ready, so Brutus keeps his cool while you two heat things up. Don't worry, with a little bit of time and a few bribes, he'll soon forget all about you two. Kiss your troubles good-bye!

Zelda

Princesses

Life with a princess can be a ROYAL pain in the @$$!

Dear Zelda,

My daughter, who is sixteen, is under the impression that everyone around her is only there to make sure she is catered to. I admit that she is spoiled (we just bought her a new BMW for her sweet sixteen) and she shops like a Hollywood glamour girl. She hardly listens to anything we say and just brushes us off like we're a waste of her valuable (nonworking) time.

I know it's partially our fault, but she's an only child and sometimes I feel bad that we didn't have another child for her to play with growing up. She'll be going away to college soon, and I'm completely fearful that she will be lost. Do you have any advice for damage control?

The Queen Mother

Dear Queen Mother,

Never fear, you're not alone! "Spoiled only-child syndrome" is common. Lots of parents overcompensate for having only one child by lavishing them with treats, treats, and more treats. However, a lollipop at the supermarket checkout line just doesn't cut it with sixteen-year-olds, and you're beginning to see how these gifts have skewed her view of the world. We sometimes forget that money doesn't always buy happiness, and at times it can even create . . . well, princesses.

It's important to remember that your royal treatment of her won't do her any favors in the long run. Once she leaves your home as an adult, she's in for a rude awakening. The world doesn't take kindly to too many princesses. As her parents, what you owe her instead is to teach her a healthy appreciation for the work it takes to afford the finer things in life, and that kindness to others will serve her well. (Why else do you think Oscar winners are always thanking the "little people"?)

So, good news! You're actually in control, even if you don't realize it, and you still have a few years to remove that tiara. You own her car, her bedroom, her clothes, and most likely the cash in her bulging wallet. I'm not saying it will be easy, and she may resent being gradually dethroned and living the life of a mere mortal. But instead of taking away all her things (which would be unfair—you did give them to her), make her earn her next rewards. New shoes? Wash the dishes. Movie money? Mow the lawn. Put in place a set of consequences to use when she disrespects you, her friends, a waiter . . . anyone. And if all else fails, pop in *Cinderella* or *Snow White* to remind her that what makes a princess most lovely is her humility.

Be strong! Making her work for what she wants may cause conflict . . . but will also turn her from a "princess" into a "priceless person." Now *that* is a no-bull cause.

Zelda

Rejection

Before you find your prince . . . you'll have to kiss a lot of frogs!

Dearest Zelda,

I have a friend who is chronically single. She's a great girl with good "everything." Good body, personality, career, house—she has it all. I've been trying to get a date with her for the last year. We play this game where she flirts ferociously with me yet she never accepts an invite to go anywhere. I'm ready, willing, and able at any time, but all this rejection is wearing me down. Sometimes I think it's just a game and she's just playing me for a fool. Am I nothing but a benchwarmer to her?

Time-Out

Dear Time-Out,

I think it's time for a huddle, and I'm calling a "flirting foul"!

In case you haven't read the whole playbook, let me clue you in about something that holds true for both dogs and people: When it comes to love, some of them can't resist a game of chase. Of course, chase is no different from any other game you've ever played. One person wins . . . and one person loses. That's why it's a game.

Unfortunately, unlike most games, which end when the buzzer sounds, this one can go on endlessly with the winner manipulating the other poor, unsuspecting players with only the slightest effort. In this game, a simple "hello," a hug, or even a tilt of the head, delivered in just the right manner, can shatter the other player, rendering him or her defenseless.

It should be clear by this point that this is not a fun game to play. Swallowing rejections and evasions for an entire year is reason enough to find a new teammate and leave that old player for some new, unsuspecting opponent. As you begin to pursue free-agent status, however, beware. Girls like your "friend" may thrive on your attention, and as she feels your flame beginning to cool, her flirtation may climb to new heights in an attempt to lure you back into dependent puppy-dog status. Keep your guard up . . . it's the oldest play in the book.

You deserve better, and it will come. And you've answered your own question: "Time-Out" is the perfect name . . . and the perfect plan.

Zelda

Retirement

Whatever happened to the good old days?

Dear Zelda,

The zip seems to have gotten stuck on my husband's zipper. Last year he retired from a company where he had worked for twenty-five years. They had a big party for him and gave him a gold watch. We had always talked about the fun we would have when we retired, but all he does now is sit at home and watch sports on television. Our sex life is next to nothing, and since I quit my job as a nurse, I have nothing to do. Retirement is worse than working. I love the advice you've been giving to people, so give me some.

Zipless Marriage

Dear Zipless Marriage,

For a long time I thought to "retire" was to get new wheels. The more I think about it, the more I believe that's what retirement should be. It seems like you and your husband are still running on those old treads. Maybe you don't go to a job anymore, but you haven't purchased any "new wheels" either, and you're not going anyplace until you do.

Retirement should be fun; it should be the fulfillment of dreams. So why don't you and your husband sit down and make a list of what makes you happy? Is it travel to Timbuktu or Tahiti? Is it volunteering at a nonprofit like the Humane Society so you can help others? Is it starting a new business that the two of you could run and manage? When I retire I dream of starting my own dog food company. Personally I can only imagine how much fun it would be cavorting around cases of kibble.

As for the stuck zipper, my guess is that when you add fun back into your life the zipper will start to move again all by itself. If not, there are terrific counselors and weekend counseling retreats out there that can work wonders. In fact, one of my friends just returned from a retreat and can't stop talking about the fun he and his wife had. They're in their fifties and recognized the importance of continually improving their relationship. And, hot dawg, they did.

So go out and replace those old tires with a set of new wheels and map out a future that will be fun and fulfilling. Get yourselves back on the road again.

Zelda

P.S. If nothing is getting your husband interested, you should consider whether he is depressed. Depression is common after retirement and often goes undiagnosed because people are reluctant to discuss it, or attribute their unhappiness to other causes. To find out more about depression and its relationship with retirement, check out the National Institute of Mental Health at: www.nimh.nih.gov/healthinformation/depoldermenu.cfm.

Risk Taking

Leap and a net will appear.

Dear Zelda,

So you are the Queen of Canines! I am a wannabe Zelda. I live with a family in Dumas, Arkansas. How can I get out of Arkansas and into the fast track of New York and L.A.? I'm a gorgeous shar-pei. My name is Lola and I know I can become a "queen" if given the opportunity. Tell me how you did it. Can I hope to hit the big time?

Lola . . . the Queen in Waiting

Dear Lola,

You flatter me. I'm really not the Queen of Canines. But I'm definitely the Queen of Me.

In my opinion, anybody can be the queen of whatever their hearts desire. If you want to go big time, set your sights and tell the world to get ready. If you've got greatness inside you, you'll find ample opportunity to unleash it on the world. A great photographer and a plugged-in PR person are de rigueur. Once you have your professional photos you need to send them to the creative directors at advertising agencies. A good creative director will recognize your big-time bowwow!

And by the way, I don't live in New York or L.A., and I didn't have to turn my back on my family to get to where I am now. Bloom where you're planted, Queen Lola. With your beauty and your regal attitude, the eyes of the world will be upon you soon enough. Just remember to be nice to everybody on your way up.

Zelda

Self Promotion

Overweight, wrinkles, double chin, unsightly facial hair . . .
if things don't improve, how will I get a date this weekend?

Dear Zelda,

I am a young, up-and-coming supervisor in the
hospitality industry. How do I keep an
overbearing coworker (who has *no* authority)
out of my way when I am trying to run
things calmly? She is *always* in everyone
else's business and conversations and is
demeaning and loud in confrontations with
other coworkers. I think it's the military
in her. Don't get me wrong: She has a lot
of job knowledge and respects me—just not
my position. Help, Zelda!

Not So Bossy About Being the Boss

Dear Not So Bossy,

Think hospitality! It's your field. How you deal with your coworker is going to need a lot of finesse. Treat her like you would treat an unruly guest. First, be polite and explain your concerns. *Then* . . . assuming that doesn't work, meet "the military in her" with the military in you. Bark your orders. Get in her face and lay down the law. Be sure to tell her that her nosiness, hostility, and pushiness are squelching morale and giving everyone "bossed-to-the-brink" syndrome. You can be firm and direct with her without giving up your calm demeanor. If this doesn't get an "about face," present your complaints in writing to your boss and request a tribunal where you and those offended could fire charges at her. Better to be blunt than bitter. Take it from Drill Sergeant Zelda: Be tough when necessary and tender when needed.

Zelda

Shopping

When all else fails . . . go shopping.

Dear Zelda,

I like your no-nonsense answers. My wife is a shop-a-holic, and I don't know what to do. She has maxed out our credit cards buying things she doesn't need and clothes she doesn't even wear. Last week she bought five pairs of shoes, all the same style, but in different colors. We are young (in our twenties) and just starting out. We are (or at least I am) trying to save money for important things, like a down payment on a house. I'm working extra hours to help achieve our financial goals and she is sabotaging my efforts. Help me, Zelda!

Shop-a-holic's Spouse

Dear Spouse,

I did some sole-searching and found seven pairs of shoes in the same style in my closet. But, as my owner reminds me every time she steers me away from the ice cream bars, I'm a model. What's your wife's excuse?

Here's my guess: She's using shopping to fill a sad and empty place in her heart. Do you think perhaps she's feeling neglected by you? You mentioned "our" financial goals. How much input did you get from her when drawing up those goals? And was it her idea to have you working all the time during the exciting first years of your marriage?

As I tell Zoe and ZeeZee every time they try to hog the whole couch, sometimes you've just got to budge for somebody else. A little budging is in order for both of you. Your wife definitely needs to budge by changing her shop-a-holic ways and being more considerate of financial goals that you establish *together*. You need to budge by being more considerate of her need for your companionship and attention. Try the "budge and budget plan." And if you're looking for something to do that doesn't cost any money, why don't you cuddle up on your couch together and watch *The Suze Orman Show*? Suze gives great tips on how to get your financial house in order.

Zelda

Sibling Rivalry

Sisters are forever.

Dear Zelda,

In your photos you seem to work well with your canine companions. Do you have any advice for a human who has a sister who continues to compete with her? My sister continues to try to one-up me and is only happy when she wins and I lose. I'd like her to be my friend, but our relationship has been made worse by parents who encouraged us to compete against each other. Help!

Sister-in-Need

Dear Sister-in-Need,

Help is here. Sibling rivalry is rarely a result of spontaneous combustion. Parents lay the kindling, strike the match, and keep fueling the flames. Parenthood can be heavy . . . very heavy. Moms and dads unknowingly breed competitiveness if they compare siblings with each other or jump in every time siblings have a conflict. Parents who do this need to be fixed. Here's what I'd do: Buy or check out a copy of the best-selling book *Siblings Without Rivalry: How to Help Your Children Live Together So You Can Live Too* by Adele Faber and Elaine Mazlish. Have your parents read it. Hold a family bull session and focus on the reasons for this competitiveness. Write down your concerns, and then brainstorm together some effective ways to generate goodwill between you and your sister.

In the meantime, when your sis starts to one-up you, don't play the game. Instead, catch her off guard by giving her a compliment or pat on the back. When you're wrong . . . admit it. When you're right . . . remain silent. Compete only with yourself; be humble, tolerant, and hopeful. Keep a stiff lower lip and stay in control. Zoe, ZeeZee, and I are rooting for you.

Zelda

Stress

There is no stress in the world. Only people thinking stressful thoughts.

Dear Zelda,

I'm a teenager who has a ton of stress. At school I feel out of place sometimes. I have a lot of friends, but when people (not my friends) look at me they give me this very strange look, like they're telling me to go away or something. I also get a lot of stress from how much work I have to do! My project partner doesn't like to do her share of the work and we are working on something that is so big that it will determine our grade for the whole semester! I don't want to fail! Is there a good way to get rid of stress? What should I do about my partner? Please share your wisdom with me!

Stressed Dude

Dear Stressed,

Leers from peers can be tough to take, but you're tougher! Walk on by with your head held high. In the big picture called "life" you can't please everyone, nor should you try. Hey, be happy you have a lot of friends and focus on them.

As for your project partner, little "Miss Understood the Assignment" who seems to be idling while you're doing all the driving, I suggest you sit down with her and list all of the things each of you need to do in order to finish the project by the deadline. I'd let her know that if she doesn't switch into high gear and complete her responsibilities, you'll have to ask your teacher for some advice. Perhaps that will rev her up. It's my guess that your teacher already knows you're behind the wheel and your partner is just along for the ride.

Now, about getting rid of stress. That's a universal problem for everyone, me included. I solve my stress by sleeping. You, however, may need to put a little more balance in your life by including time for fun, eating nutritious food (I include ice cream in that category), and getting some exercise (one sit-up and I'm finished, but do what you can). There is a great book to read called *Don't Sweat the Small Stuff for Teens: Simple Ways to Keep Your Cool in Stressful Times* by Richard Carlson. The road to adulthood is full of bumps, dips, curves, and forks. Sounds like you're doing an awesome job of steering in the right direction. The best part of the ride lies ahead, so stay positive and persevere. Survival is hanging on after others let go.

Zelda

Success

If you want to be top dog, you've got to get off the porch.

Dear Zelda,

My name is Bubba. I'm a big, buff bulldog and I've followed your career and success. I want to know how being a "top dog" has changed your life. Do you get a special diet? Do you ride in limousines and have pedicures and spa treatments? Actually, I'd like to be your boyfriend. Any chance?

Luva Bubba

Dear Luva Bubba,

Being a top dog does have its advantages, but don't let the glitz and glamour blind you. Underneath my movie star . . . well, Rubenesque looks, sharp comedic wit, and "leopard-loud" style lies a simple gal with simple values and simple dreams. Sure, my diet consists of special bulldog food from Royal Canin (what else would a queen eat?), and I have had my share of limousine and jet rides (to *The Oprah Winfrey Show*, *Good Morning America*, and *Martha Stewart*), but those are just part of the territory. At home I keep it real. Zoe, ZeeZee, and I like to ride in a safe yet practical Jeep with canine cushions, seat belts, and fully stocked un-tip-a-bull water bowls.

As for pedicures and spa treatments . . . every girl who was brought up right knows that it's a cardinal rule that you don't leave the house without perfect pedi'd paws. Spas I can do without. If I wanted to roll around in mud with cucumbers on my face and seaweed hangin' out of spots where no one should . . . well, never mind.

I would have to say that my favorite thing about becoming a top dog, and I mean this sincerely, is the opportunity to meet and get to know the thousands of friends who have contacted me since this started. Any top dog knows that without the love and support of friends and family and enormous amounts of mutual respect . . . you just end up being a "dawg" on top.

Oh, and one last thing, Bubba: You can be "one" of my boyfriends anytime! XOXO!

Zelda

Superwomen

Behind every superman . . . is a superwoman.

Dear Zelda,

I see that your column is on "superwomen."
I want to be one! What is it that makes
a woman a superwoman?

Mere Mortal

Dear Mere Mortal,

For everyone, not just women, this is a great question. Without a doubt, I would say the "it" that turns mere mortals into superwomen is "confidence."

Sure, there are numerous other factors that go into the making of a superwoman: intelligence, charisma, drive, determination, etc., but without the confidence to convey those factors, the traits of a superwoman may lay dormant, never to realize their full potential. A woman who walks into a room without confidence is merely that . . . a woman who walks into a room.

Give that same woman a confident walk, a confident look, and the inner confidence that radiates like an aura around her, and that woman becomes a presence. A superwoman doesn't leap tall buildings, she enters them like she owns them. A superwoman doesn't stop a speeding locomotive with her bare hands, she stops traffic with a walk of easy confidence. The most powerful superpower a superwoman can possess is that she doesn't have to be all things to all people. She has the confidence to know when enough is enough without guilt or reservations.

The main misconception most people have about superwomen is that they do everything (and I know some who do), but what's really important is not necessarily that they *do* everything, it's that they know they *can* do *anything*. It's easy to be intimidated by the world, by the skills of others, and by our own doubts, and it's hard to remember just how capable we are, and the things we can accomplish when we set our minds to it.

You wonder what it is that will make you a superwoman. You already have it. You just have to learn how to embrace it and exude it.

Zelda

Survival

I'd never vote you . . . off my island.

Dear Zelda,

I hate my job! I don't want to get out of bed in the morning. I work for a family-owned and -run business and, while my salary is okay, I feel there is no way I will ever get ahead. My problem is that I like the family who owns the business. I grew up with their children, who now also work for the company. They refer to me as their surrogate son. I'm in charge of about twenty people and I don't enjoy hiring and firing them. How do I get out and stay friends with the family? Any suggestions?

Fear of Family

Dear Fear of Family,

We're not talking about the Corleone family, are we? (I want to make sure before I start dolin' out the advice, as no one wants to sleep with the fishes!) Personally, I've never met a bed I wanted to get out of. However, not wanting to get out of bed because you can't stand the thought of going to your job is a whole different story.

Working for a family-owned business and not being part of *la famiglia* can have its disadvantages. In a perfect world, the "surrogate son" would be valued and appreciated just as much for his hard work as the blood relative who may (or may not!) be putting in the same effort. But most family businesses are not a perfect world. Still, the fact that they've put you in charge of twenty people shows an incred-i-bull amount of trust and respect, and it's probably not to be taken lightly. Just remember, to get ahead in any working environment, there will be times when you have to do things that you don't like.

You have to decide whether you dislike the job itself or the fact that your options for upward growth are limited. If you don't like the job, it's time for a change. Be honest and straightforward with the family in saying that you are grateful for all they have done for you, but you are interested in trying something else.

If, however, the work itself is okay, but you feel a little claustrophobic in the three-ring family circus, you might try to move up before you decide to move out: Talk to someone in the family about your concerns and come up with specific suggestions for what they might do to meet your needs. If they are willing to make some reasonable compromises, great! If not, they will know that you respected them enough to try to work it out, but that you also have to meet your own needs, direct your own life, and ride your own hog.

Since you like the family you work for, it may be worth trying to work it out. Finding a job you like is hard, but finding a job you like with people you like is even harder. If this family really does consider you one of their own, they will understand and support your decision. Arrivederci!

Zelda

Take the Plunge

Go ahead . . . take the plunge!

Dear Zelda,

I am in the last year of my forties. I've always played it safe and admire those who take chances. My alter ego keeps telling me to take chances and add some excitement and adventure in my life. I think my fiftieth birthday would be a great place to start. I have been inspired by your words of wisdom and would welcome advice to get me outside my little box.

Boxed In

Dear Boxed In,

Fifty times around the sun, a fabulous accomplishment! That may seem like a lot, but just think: When I turn fifty, in dog years I'll be *three hundred* and fifty! Your fifty doesn't sound so bad by comparison.

It's never too late to grab life by the throttle. Playing it safe can only get you so far, and it takes a lot of courage to step outside the safe, comfortable routines of life. The first step is often the hardest, so make up your mind, formulate a concrete plan, and then just *do it*! Of course, there's risk taking, and then there's risk taking: taking salsa lessons, traveling somewhere exotic, or writing a novel? *Hot*! Investing your entire nest egg into a startup dot-com whose mascot is a sock puppet? *Not*!

What kind of risks do *you* want to take? Tired of the desk job and always wanted to try your hand at being a glassblower? Find some glassblowers in your area and discover what it takes to get your feet wet and your glass melting. Or maybe you have some dormant talent like juggling. Join a group, meet like-minded individuals on a public forum like Craigslist (www.craigslist.org), or just start your own group! Or perhaps you're feeling a little more adventurous and want to hike the Inca Trail, raft the Grand Canyon, or do some international volunteer work. Check out a professional adventure company like Backroads (www.backroads.com). You're only limited by your imagination.

Make a list of the big priorities in your life, and another list of wonderful fantasies you've always dreamed about. Then think about how to make those fantasies happen. As long as you make responsible decisions for yourself or those people who love you and depend on you, the sky's the limit!

We bulldogs are big risk takers: We were originally bred to face off against angry, full-grown bulls about fifty times our size. So the next time the big risks in your life seem impossible or particularly scary, just think of how my great-great-great-great grandfathers must have felt stepping into the bullpen! Leap, and a net will appear!

Zelda

Tough Decisions

Tough decision? Take time to "mullet" over.

Dear Zelda,

My wife and I have been married over twenty years. Our two children are in college. The other day I was in a bookstore and saw a title that stopped me in my tracks. It said *Too Good to Leave, Too Bad to Stay*. I immediately thought of my marriage. My wife and I live under the same roof but don't share the same interests anymore. She likes to stay home, watch television, and visit with her friends on the phone. Now that the children aren't home, I'd like to travel and see a lot of the world we couldn't afford to see when the children were little. We don't seem to want to spend time together, and the children are the only things we share. Am I being selfish to think that maybe we should separate and find new friends and/or partners, or should we stay married and keep the family together?

Too Good to Leave, Too Bad to Stay

Dear Too Good to Leave, Too Bad To Stay,

Selfish? Absolutely not. At what age and after how many years do we stop, take a deep breath, look around, and say, "Is this it? Is this really the rest of my life?"

Many people experience empty-nest syndrome. After waving good-bye to that last child and wishing them well with their lifelong ambitions, many people turn around to face the person they've been living with for so many years and realize they have no idea who he or she is. Your last child left, and it feels like they took with them every last drop of glue that was keeping the family together.

This is a time when people often reevaluate their goals, wishes, relationships, and senses of identity. I can't give you easy answers about whether to separate or to stay together. Often we feel oppressed by others' expectations—that we are supposed to love someone, or that we have to stay together for the family. These pressures can sink even the most seaworthy of relationships. The truth is you really don't have to do these things anymore. But before you run off with your dental hygienist in your new Porsche, let me try and introduce you to someone you might find very special.

Allow me to introduce . . . your wife. If you haven't met her recently, she was the face you couldn't forget and the love you would never regret. You were soul mates. In fact, she was so perfect, you just had to marry her. You didn't state in your letter that you didn't still love her. Before you do anything, make an honest effort to get reacquainted. She's probably fallen into the same rut, forgetting all the wonderful qualities that first brought you together.

Start simple, and don't underestimate the power of memories—they can help ignite the flames that warmed your hearts and fueled your fires. Try something different, fun, and away from home (and the TV and phone). Propose a late-night drive on a warm, sultry evening, or a sweet dessert and warm coffee at your old favorite haunt, and see where it leads. We tend to take for granted those things that are right in front us, yet once gone, they may forever be un-retrieve-a-bull.

Zelda

Tough Times

Tough times never last . . . tough people do!

Dear Zelda,

I think I'm in one of the toughest times I'll ever be in. My two labs, Salt and Pepper, are fourteen and a half years old and not doing so well. They are both having a terrible time walking and getting around, even to go to the bathroom. They've been together since they were puppies. Salt is worse off than Pepper, and my vet (whom I've had for the same amount of time) says he'll have to be put down fairly soon. Since they both have such problems walking and they've been together so long, he suggested that they both be put down at the same time. He says that Pepper won't go on much longer once Salt is gone, and he'd probably be happier going with her, rather than dying with a broken heart. I know it's for the best, but I'm devastated. Do all dogs really go to heaven?

Friend in Need

Dear Friend in Need,

I'm so sorry to hear about Salt and Pepper. It sounds like they've both had long and wonderful lives with you, and with each other, and a dog can't ask for much more than that. The average dog lives only to be about thirteen, so Salt and Pepper have definitely beaten the odds (and then some). That's due in no small part to the love and care they must have felt from you all their lives.

As for whether or not all dogs go to heaven . . . I sometimes try and imagine what heaven would be like for us dogs: exploring a park with miles of lush green lawn and fire hydrants behind every corner, or finding a huge bone to settle down and chew on, or being curled up by the fire with our dog friends and our family surrounding us. That's when I realize that we dogs *do* get to go to heaven, because if we're lucky and we end up in families like yours, we actually get to experience it every day.

We have simple pleasures, and hopefully you will rest a little easier knowing that Salt and Pepper have truly been in heaven all their lives with you. It's sad to say good-bye to us, and it's sad for us to say good-bye too, but in this world there is no improving on a life well lived among friends and family.

It sounds like it's time to let them go. I think your veterinarian is right that it's only fair to let them share their whole lives together, including the end. Our thoughts are with you as you go through this difficult time—this inevitable part of life. All parents dream that their children will grow up to live full and happy lives, and at fourteen and a half, Salt and Pepper can rest together peacefully now, their lives full of love from each other and from you. Heartfelt wishes from all of us here.

Zelda

Toxic Relationships

Maybe if I just close my eyes . . . he'll go away.

Dear Zelda,

What am I to do? The man in my life is constantly criticizing me. Everything I do is wrong. I can't seem to make him happy. He told me he thought my hair was "mousy brown," so I became a blonde. Now he tells me I look like a "cheap blonde." The worst thing is that he makes fun of me in front of our friends. I'm afraid to leave him and afraid to stay. Any advice?

Tears on My Pillow

Dear Tears on My Pillow,

This time dye your hair red. Why? Not to please your ungrateful man but to get a taste of a redhead's temper. Maybe then you could tell your beau what you really think of his insulting treatment of you. Honey, the only thing a doormat is good for is wiping muddy paws. Don't be this guy's doormat. If you are afraid to stand up to him now, start building up your courage so you'll be brave enough to tell him off, leave him, or possibly both when the time comes.

Understand that it is okay to have opposing views, and it is equally okay to express them. Hold your ground and practice being assertive. He is pushing you into submission in order to feel validated.

I recommend that you read the book *Feel the Fear and Do It Anyway* by Susan Jeffers, Ph.D. It's for people who know in their hearts what they should do but just need a little nudge. If you also read *Verbal Abuse Survivors Speak Out on Relationship and Recovery* by Patricia Evans, you'll see you're not alone and that there are ways to get out of an abusive situation. You can conquer almost any fear, so don't sit home and think about it. Go out and get busy. With dogged determination, you can defeat your self-doubt and fear. Dry your tears and pull yourself out from underneath this man. You're one bright blonde for taking action by asking for advice.

Zelda

Trouble

When you're in deep water the best thing to do is shut your mouth.

Dear Zelda,

My mother-in-law is driving me crazy. She is always telling me better ways to do everything: how to make a better meatloaf, what color looks best on me, which wine to serve, how I might lose a little weight, etc. My husband and I have been married only two years, but I want to tell her to zip her lip, and I know that isn't respectful. What would you do?

Mother-in-loathe

Dear Mother-in-loathe,

Take comfort in the fact that by facing the harsh scrutiny of your in-laws, you are joining a long and proud legacy that stretches back as far as people have been getting hitched. Some of the earliest cave paintings were apparently just nasty cartoons of mothers-in-law! The truth is, when you marry your husband, you marry his family. Without realizing it, you accepted this woman as part of your family during your wedding vows . . . for better or, in this case, for *worse*!

Just because she's family doesn't mean you have to take her abuse. Of course, she thinks that she's just trying to help, and that her words of wisdom are only meant to better your life and help your marriage (she's *sooooo* thoughtful). You married her baby, and her baby deserves the best. What she doesn't understand is that he picked you because he thought *you* were the best.

The good news is I've got it covered! Coincidentally, that's also my advice to you: When you need to make a better meatloaf . . . "*Oh*, no thanks, I've got it covered." When she suggests a different wine . . . "*Oh*, no thanks . . . I've got it covered." Chartreuse is really your color (absolutely untrue unless you're a snow pea) . . . again . . . "No thanks, I've got it covered." A simple "thanks" followed by the fact that you appreciate the advice, but you've "got it covered," is a polite way of letting her know that you are a grown woman capable of making your own decisions.

The only challenge is that she obviously wants to be a part of your life, and "having it covered" about everything she brings up is bound to make her feel shut out. Try to redirect her energies and attentions in more positive directions. For example, if you know she loves to garden, go out of your way to ask her for recommendations on plantings for this spring. If you build a positive relationship where she is able to have input into some parts of your life, it may then be easier to get her to keep her nose out of other parts.

I've always said, "If it's not one thing . . . it's your mother (in-law)."

Zelda

When to Quit?

When you're up to your ears in alligators . . . it's time to drain the swamp!

Dear Zelda,

I earn tons of money but hate my job. I work for a company that asks me to help promote products that I think are harmful to whoever consumes them. I'm talking about selling sugary soft drinks to teenagers. I'm having nightmares about graveyards filled with rotting teeth and teenagers. On one hand, I have a big mortgage payment every month and on the other, I have a conscience that won't let me sleep. Give me some of your solid canine advice, Zelda.

Drowning in Indecision . . .
Alligators at My Ears

Dear Drowning in Indecision,

Swampland isn't the best real estate, and alligators sure don't make the best neighbors. It sounds like your conscience is telling you it's time for a change. But however much you'd like to get out of that moral swamp, with that big mortgage breathing down your neck, you could go straight from the swamp to the street!

Before you quit your job, sniff around and see if there is another job in your company where you would feel better, perhaps promoting a different product. Do they also distribute natural juices or healthy foods? If so, go to whoever assigns positions and products and let them know your interests and concerns. Before you go, make sure you have concrete suggestions about resolving the situation by switching to an account that excites you and that you would be proud to promote.

Me? Every night I drool about promoting a dog food company: I'm already their test market! If, however, you are stuck in your present position, don't burn any bridges. Fend off those alligators with a friendly smile while looking outside your company for a job that reflects your beliefs and interests. You must meet the mortgage payments, and finding a new job is a lot easier if you are presently employed, especially at a high salary. Go online, go to a headhunter, and get in touch with companies you admire. Keep looking and don't be afraid to ask. If you don't ask, the answer will always be "no." You are well-paid now, and that means another company is likely to recognize your talents and abilities. Sometimes you just have to look and wait for the right opportunity.

Once you've found your new home, try to leave your old one on good terms. Even alligators like to party, so throw a "moving on" party, and try not to tell your colleagues how morally reprehensible you think they are. At least you know there will be plenty of soft drinks at the party! Better to leave the alligators well-fed than fed-up.

Zelda

The Work-a-Day World

It's not how people deal with you, it's how you deal with people.

Dear Zelda,

How should I keep from letting coworkers' bad moods affect me? Also, sometimes I deal with difficult or rude customers; how can I learn to shrug it off? Thanks in advance. I know you'll be able to help me.

Woe at the Workplace

Dear Woe at the Workplace,

Whenever possible, put some space between you and sourpusses. No matter where you work, grouch gurus can infest morale and test your tolerance level. These grumps may feel insecure, unappreciated, resentful, or simply apathetic. Never take it personally. As challenging as it might be, come across as being upbeat and enthusiastic. Look for the good, not the growly. Get in the habit of being compassionate with rude, abrasive customers. They could be having an underdog day. Never argue with a skunk. Concentrate on being a good listener and practice daily patience and forgiveness. Apply a sense of humor to bad situations. He who laughs . . . lasts. After difficult moments, take some deep breaths. Indulge in mini-meditation breaks. According to Sandra Crowe, author of *Since Strangling Isn't an Option: Dealing with Difficult People—Common Problems and Uncommon Solutions* (which I highly recommend), as much as 75 percent of our stress comes from just having our eyes open. So shut them!

Smile if you want a smile from another face. Accept that some days in any workplace can just be a *royal pain*! Two other books to consider are *Get Along with Anyone, Anytime, Anywhere: Eight Keys to Creating Enduring Connections with Customers, Coworkers . . . Even Kids* by Arnold Sanow and Sandra Strauss and *Undress Your Stress: Thirty Curiously Fun Ways to Take Off Tension* by Lois Levy. Switch your attitude from "I have to go to work" to "I want to go to work." Every day is a new adventure! If nothing improves after all is said and tried, dig around for a new gig.

Zelda

Workplace Woes

Don't let others slow you down.

Dear Zelda,

I work with two women who hate each other. They are both very difficult people and hard to deal with individually, but I do get along with both of them because I am not the confrontational type and try to get along with everyone. Granted, we have had disagreements, but we have gotten over them and we go on. These two ladies will never get along, and I have never seen such hate between two people. They are making my dream job a total nightmare. I have gone to my supervisor, but she will not do anything about the mean things they say and do to each other. Have any suggestions other than find a new job?

Girl in the Middle

Dear Girl in the Middle,

I hate it when cats fight. Especially when it's under my window and I'm trying to sleep. Talk about nightmares!

Don't let the cat fight in your office chase you away from your dream job. Whenever they push each other's buttons, press your delete key. They can't "make" your dream job a nightmare without your consent. Regardless, their constant bickering can potentially take its toll on the productivity and well-being of the entire workplace. If you join forces with other bothered employees and take this problem back to your supervisor, maybe a team approach would wake your supervisor up. Before you do, however, document the facts of their disputes and how your performance, morale, and motivation have been impacted. Perhaps if you begin by pointing out to your supervisor the benefits of a copasetic workplace (higher productivity, less sick time, etc.), she will be more likely to perk up her ears.

Until your supervisor works magic and gets the gals to settle down, you can try figuring out how to add some frivolity to the mix. When you're around these women, smile big and be fun loving. Slip them some *Dilbert* cartoons or a copy of *Zelda's Survival Guide*. Humor can soften any hate. If your supervisor continues to miss the message, forward it to the Human Resources department. Since conflict is a catalyst for change, maybe one of them will simply up and quit, be transferred, or be fired. In the meantime, be prepared. You never know when you might have to separate those two cats yourself!

Zelda

Worry

Worry is today's mouse eating tomorrow's cheese.

Dear Zelda,

Every morning I put my six-year-old son on the school bus. I'm a single mom who has to work, so I can't take him to school. From the minute he steps on that bus until the minute he gets home, I worry. He's so little and fragile, and the thought of any harm coming to him makes me feel sick and terrified. How does a mother get past all the worrying? Does it ever end?

Scared of the School Bus . . .
and Everything Else

Dear Scared of the School Bus,

A mother never stops worrying . . . she just learns to cope with it. Take heart—the worries don't just go away, but it does get easier, and you will learn to relax. By your third child you'll be suggesting they just hitchhike.

   We all have to learn to let go of our children, and unless you plan on shadowing him every day, there's no way of making absolutely sure that nothing will ever happen to him. Going to school, staying at a friend's house, and playing in the park are all part of the journey of growing up, and it does require leaving the nest, at least for a few hours a day. This separation helps little, fragile tykes turn into strong, independent adults.

   As a kid, enjoying activities without your overprotective (and I mean that in the nicest way) mother teaches you to become more outgoing, confident, and aware of your surroundings. This doesn't mean buying him a ticket to Vegas for next weekend, but it does mean letting him go play in the mud, get a few scrapes, and solve some problems for himself.

   Your strong smile and happy wave as he leaves on the bus each morning will help him feel comfortable and confident. Today he may seem fragile and little, but you have to realize that someday he will be bigger, and hopefully a little less fragile. He's going to have to do a lot of growing on his own. The important thing is to always keep your bond with him strong and the lines of communication open. Knowing you trust him (even if you're secretly terrified!) will make him feel more comfortable telling you what he's up to. You're a loving mother, and you'll always worry . . . it's a natural instinct! The secret is to keep reminding yourself that these fears are all part of the process of growing up, for both of you.

   Remember that birds make small nests for a reason, and young things will let you know when they're ready for that push. Worry won't give your son strong wings, but love and trust will.

Zelda

You're Hired!
You're hired!

Dear Zelda,

Big dilemma here. I just started a new job with a great company. All of us are in cubicles, and mine happens to be next to a girl who is *very* popular (I know this because her cell phone rings all day long with personal calls that start before I can even sip my morning coffee). I like her but the constant ringing is driving me crazy and making it hard to concentrate. I feel like complaining to the boss is a bad idea since I'm the new girl (which is a nickname I get to hear over and over). How do I shut off her gossipy cell phone?

Help Wanted

Dear Help Wanted,

I have to agree, there is nothing worse than getting to work, sugar-free vanilla nonfat latte in hand, and suddenly being startled by an annoying ringtone and the high-pitched banshee wail of "*Oh my God, you are kidding!*" from the adjacent cube. Not even the best gossip should be heard before morning lattes.

Cell's bells . . . she's taken the phrase "Can you hear me now?" to a whole new level. This is a place of business, not a sorority house (well . . . unless you're actually working at a sorority house). Maybe that's why your cubicle was empty to begin with. She ran the last one out of there faster than she could burn up her monthly minutes. Don't delay, sister, *mute* her. Just because your cubicles are adjacent doesn't mean you have to be "cell-mates."

Start simply with a gentle knock on her cubicle wall and ask her politely if she could turn down her cell ringer or put it on vibrate. Tell her, respectfully but directly, that otherwise it's hard for you to carry on a conversation with clients. Hopefully she will understand your desire for a professional space, and that not everyone wants to hear the ringtone version of "Girls Just Wanna Have Fun" every waking minute.

If that doesn't work, or if the direct approach is not your style, you could try to teach an old dog a new trick by showing her how to text message or instant message. Just slip into the conversation how easy it is to text with friends, how you do it all the time, and how cool it is. Or, you could just drop a leaflet about texting or instant messaging on her chair anonymously.

Finally, if all your efforts have not managed to quiet the morning fanfare, go to the big kahuna. I'm guessing that if you can hear her ringing ruckus, so can everyone else, and that the boss is probably already aware of your gossip guru and her loud mobile. It may require new office rules about cell phone use, and that's where the head honcho comes in, hopefully taking some of the pressure off of you.

Offices should be fun and social places, but you still deserve your peace and quiet! Don't let this diva of deafening dialogue "cell" your morning short.

Zelda

Zeal

The person who has no fire in himself can't ignite others.

Dear Zelda,

I work for a really boring company doing really boring work. I hate getting out of bed in the morning and nothing excites me. Do you have any suggestions to kick-start me into action? I feel like a slug going nowhere.

Stuck in a Rut

Dear Stuck in a Rut,

Work matters, and it takes up a huge amount of time in our lives . . . so it's worth finding something that excites you or that gets you out of bed in the morning. It doesn't matter what it is. It just matters that you care about it, that you're satisfied by it (at least sometimes), and that you wake up ready to do it. If there is one thing we dogs know, it's that nothing is very exciting until you start chasing it.

Everyone always *says* they'd like to do something that matters, but we've all got bills to pay, groceries to buy, and dogs to feed (priority number one!). In fact, there *is* a lot of practical stuff that needs taking care of, and I'm not suggesting you quit tomorrow and invest your entire nest egg into self-producing your debut smooth jazz album. There are practical jobs that can satisfy you, and there are probably even ways to get more satisfaction out of your current job.

Start by thinking of the things in your life that bring you some satisfaction. Take a long hard look at your prior professional experiences and try to learn about your capabilities and your passions from things you have excelled at in the past. Use this to steer a course for your career and angle toward something better. Still drawing a blank? Then maybe it's time to start thinking about a career change.

I can't tell you what to do with your life, but I can tell you that you're the one who has to make it happen, and until you realize it, you'd better get mighty comfy in that rut. You'd be in good company; many people get permanently stuck in ruts because they're absolutely positive that some amazing change is going to come knocking on their door. It can take years for them to figure out that it rarely happens.

Create your own excitement, and remember, without risk there are no rewards, and without rewards . . . there are only more ruts.

Zelda

Advice is what we ask for when we
already know the answer but wish we didn't.

—Erica Jong